T0274589

THE
HERBAL
ARTS

*A Handbook of Plant
Magic, Folklore,
Recipes, Spells, &
Charms*

About the Author

Patricia Telesco has been a part of the Neo-Pagan community for over 30 years. During her speaking engagements across the U.S., Trish met many wise people working behind the scenes who blessed her with down-to-earth perspectives for going forward with books and life. Along the way, cooking at festivals led to writing more about culinary topics. The result has been very happy bellies for family and friends alike.

Food is love; food is hospitality. Food changes life, and life changes food.

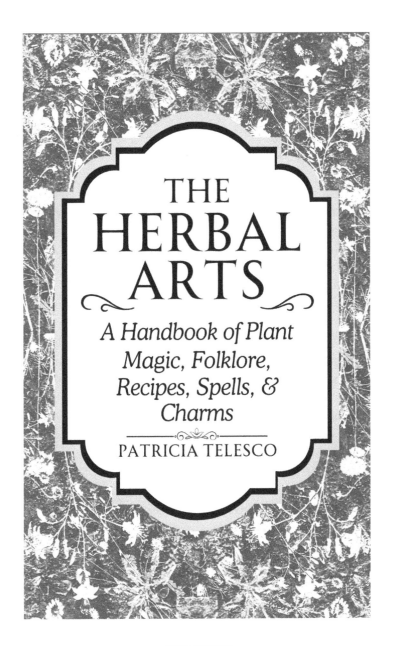

THE
HERBAL
ARTS

*A Handbook of Plant
Magic, Folklore,
Recipes, Spells, &
Charms*

PATRICIA TELESCO

Chicago, IL

Paperback ISBN: 978-1-959883-53-1
Library of Congress Control Number on file.

Published by:
Crossed Crow Books, LLC
6934 N Glenwood Ave, Suite C
Chicago, IL 60626
www.crossedcrowbooks.com

Printed in the United States of America.
IBI

With gratitude to the Earth and Mother Nature's abundantly diverse and useful supermarket, without which this book could never have been written.

"In its essential spirit, in its proper garden meaning, an herb is a garden plant which has been cherished for itself and for a use and has not come down to us as a purely decorative thing."

—Henry Beston, author of *Herbs and Earth*

Acknowledgements

Many thanks to the unknown woman I met so many years ago, making her own soap, who began what would become my lifelong adventure in herbalism.

Dave, Blythe, and my other friends whose homes become lending libraries when I'm doing research.

My family, for allowing me to give up so much of my time to the computer screen.

My readers and all the wonderful folks around the country who have been supportive. You make the magic in my life happen every day through your kindness.

Contents

ᏨᎬ Introduction ᏨᎬ

"Powerful grace that lies in herbs, plants, stones,
and their true qualities."
—William Shakespeare

Herbs are one of nature's most bountiful and beautiful blessings to humankind. Amid the variety of flora that grows unassumingly beneath our feet, one may unearth culinary herbs, healthful herbs, herbs that beautify, and herbs with aromas that uplift weary souls. Because of this diversity, herbalism has gained attention and acclaim from many people, some who don't realize that this art has a rich, long-standing tradition.

The roots of herbalism delve down into humankind's earliest history. The oldest written records on herbalism and its use come to us from China, Egypt, and India. In 200 BCE, the Chinese *Shen-nung Pen ts'ao,* or "Classic of the Materia Medica," logged over three hundred herbal formulas from as early as the third millennium BCE. An Egyptian remedial papyrus from 2000 BCE detailed even more herbs, adding regional plants, and, by 1000 BCE, the Vedic scriptures of India delved into herbalism for common applications, mixing science with myth, lore, and superstition.

These great civilizations, and many that followed, looked to nature as a representative of divine or universal patterns and, in some instances, a god. This animistic outlook developed into the *doctrine of signatures,* which lasted well into the Middle Ages.

The doctrine regards all life as part of an intricate network with the Creator placing clues about a plant's use within its appearance. For example, a yellow plant might be used as a cure for jaundice, or various seeds might be consumed to aid fertility.

From ancient tribal shamans to modern botanists, people have experimented with nearly every piece of foliage on this planet for culinary, magical, medicinal, or craft purposes. These experiments have greatly benefited the modern practitioner. Over time, herbs that worked effectively in one or more of these applications became part of oral tradition and eventually entered the general body of folk wisdom passed down through families from generation to generation. Thanks to such diligence, much of this knowledge remains with us today.

Until the advent of modern medicine, administration of the herbal arts was entrusted to the skilled hands of monks, village healers, and homemakers. Their kitchens and gardens served as the equivalent of a modern first aid kit. Since most of these people had little means, the herbal tradition was by necessity economical and pragmatic, striving ever to heal the body, soothe the spirit, and nourish the mind with readily available ingredients. In the process, nature was always honored and given its due, making herbal philosophies ecologically sound!

In writing this book, the reciprocal, practical, and everyday nature of this tradition has been kept in mind. *The Herbal Arts* is a guide for blending the best of our ancestors' discoveries and ideals with the realities, knowledge, and equipment of our modern world. History, heritage, science, and spirituality mingle harmoniously together to improve or augment many facets of daily living—from making a remedial tea to ridding a garden of pests naturally.

For those embarking on herbalism as a new adventure, Chapter One reviews fundamental information and simple procedures that make domestic herbalism more satisfying and successful. This includes what constitutes an herb in the broadest sense, where to get herbs, how to store your components, a list of useful tools, preparation instructions, and how to add a spiritual dimension to this art.

Chapter Two furnishes basic recipes for herbal edibles, soaps, bath salts, and healing preparations. Unlike the recipes in Chapter Three, these formulas are not herb specific. Instead, they provide proportions for creatively mixing herbs to reflect personal needs or goals.

Chapter Three is an herb multipedia comprised of an herbal dictionary, encyclopedia, recipe book, folklore compendium, history text, gardening advisor, and wellness guide, all rolled into one. Most of the plants listed are easily found in or around your home. Herbs with fewer applications are also described to provide a comprehensive resource for your many herbal questions. Additionally, Chapter Three quotes various herbalists, physicians, and philosophers, noting their opinions on specific plants. A "who's who" of these individuals is provided in Appendix A for your reference.

Appendix B provides a list of correspondences for a selection of herbs, flowers, trees, and vegetables, including the ruling planet, predominant element, associated gods and goddesses, and metaphysical associations. These correspondences are not necessary to successful domestic herbalism, but many early herbalists trusted in greater powers to aid their art and believed in the mystical powers of herbs. Readers who incorporate herbalism into their spiritual practices—especially in making ritual preparations such as incense, anointing oils, and libations—should find this section very helpful.

Finally, Appendix C provides a list organized alphabetically, with an herb's botanical name. Many suppliers list herbs by their botanical name, so keep Appendix C handy when shopping!

This book represents over thirteen years of study, research, trial and error, and happy puttering in my kitchen. I find herbalism to be a very enjoyable, relaxing sideline that saves money, reflects earth-friendly philosophies, encourages holistic thinking, and isn't nearly as time-consuming as one might expect. I believe you will likewise find tremendous fulfillment in having your kitchen become a haven where body, mind, and spirit are all served from one platter.

Good cooking!

Disclaimer

Herbalism is still under scientific and medical investigation. While many herbs have proven serviceable, the remedies in this book should not be used in place of medicine. Always consult a doctor when experiencing physical symptoms. The author and the publisher of this book cannot guarantee any results from historical, folkloric curatives.

1

METHODS AND MUSINGS

"What is a weed? A plant whose virtues have not been discovered."
—Ralph Waldo Emerson

"To see a World in a Grain of Sand and Heaven in a Wild Flower."
—William Blake

We live in a time when natural ways of staying fit, working the land, and caring for our homes have become almost chic. It is not surprising to find the herbal arts taking an awkward commercial role in our society, far more than they ever did before. One can hardly listen to the radio or watch television without hearing about natural vitamins or a book espousing herbal avenues to personal wellness.

This commercialization and public scrutiny have good and bad impacts. Unfortunately, the valuable hearthside heritage of this art is lost in the glitz and glamor. This creates an unrealistic image that may deter some individuals from exploring herbalism. Part of the purpose behind this chapter is to take the plastic wrapping off herbalism and bring it back to grassroots applications. The first steps are defining what constitutes an herb and obtaining the components and tools for the task at hand.

What's in a Name (When an Herb Isn't an Herb)

Despite dictionary definitions to the contrary, herbalism's scope is not confined to the realm of seed-producing annuals, biennials, or perennials whose stems wither annually. Throughout history, the beloved term *herb* has come to mean considerably more. During the Middle Ages, an era known as the *Age of Herbals*, any plant that had culinary, remedial, aromatic, veterinary, cosmetic, domestic, agrarian, or pleasurable applications was classified as an herbal. The definition was broad, encompassing trees, flowers, roots, seeds, vegetables, fruits, nuts, bushes, berries, and all their respective parts.

The reason for such variety is twofold. First, our ancestors wished to explore all corners of creation to improve their quality of life. They applied spiritual ideals to mundane needs as a practical application of the doctrine of signatures. Their work engendered hope, which is a powerful helpmate.

Secondly, our forebears were very pragmatic. Without the modern convenience of the neighborhood store or the natural food cooperative, whatever existed on the land and in the kitchen was the first logical line of experimentation. The lucky householder would have access to a trader selling foreign herbs, but they often were expensive. Most skilled herbalists wasted nothing and rarely purchased an herb unless it could be used in several compounds. For example, a unique edible flower might open the purse strings because its petals could be employed in beauty treatments, medicines, brewing, and even in preparing dinner!

By not limiting their options, our ancestors allowed nature to become an apothecary where they could shop and research liberally. Thanks to their efforts, plant curatives form the foundation of 75% of our modern medicine, and we benefit from their herbal origins, which have far fewer side effects. This is one of the many gifts from our herbal heritage to the modern hearthside herbalist, in addition to the variety of herbs on our pantry spice rack.

Growing Herbs

For those who enjoy outdoor or window box gardening, growing your own herbs will prove very satisfying. You can be sure they are free of any pesticides. Additionally, fresh herbs are available whenever you want them without running to the store!

The next step in herbal gardening is choosing the herbs to grow. Do you want healthful herbs? Culinary herbs? Dyeing herbs? A mix? Make a list of plants you would use most often, then check their necessary growing conditions in Chapter Three. For example, numerous medicinal herbs grow well in containers, including aloe, peppermint, thyme, and bay. In contrast, large plants like lavender and chamomile usually fare better outdoors. Depending on the space available and where you live, this quick review should provide an initial shopping list to follow.

Seeds and cuttings are easy to come by at home and garden centers, but read the label carefully before buying. Different seeds and cuttings need to be planted and cultivated at different times for best results. Some also need more (or less) sunshine and moisture than others.

Group herbs based on their climatic needs for planting and mark them clearly once in the ground. One leafy green can look a lot like another once everything starts growing! For soil, good potting dirt for indoor gardens should need little, if any, fertilizer. Blend outdoor dirt with some topsoil, peat moss, manure, loam, and compost from your heap. Use cedar shavings on top of this to deter weeds and some insects.

If gardening outdoors, place delicate herbs behind sturdier ones to protect them from wind. Also consider consulting a good guide to companion planting to ensure both the herbs and the soil benefit from a well-planned garden. The following chart provides a brief overview of some recommended companion plants as a reference.

Herbs		*Companion*
Anise	↔	Coriander
Basil	↔	Tomato
Borage	↔	Beans
Chamomile	↔	Onion
Chives	↔	Carrot
Chrysanthemum	↔	Lettuce
Dandelion	↔	Fruits
Dill	↔	Cabbage
Garlic	↔	Rose
Horseradish	↔	Potato
Marigold	↔	Tomato
Mint	↔	Cabbage
Mustard	↔	Grapes
Onion	↔	Strawberry
Oregano	↔	Beans
Sage	↔	Marjoram
Tarragon	↔	Vegetables
Thyme	↔	Eggplant

In colder climates, cultivate seeds inside first to get a head start on the season. When all threats of frost are gone, separate the seedlings and transplant them outside. Indoor or out, the best time to water your plants is early in the morning or close to sundown to avoid waterlogging. In areas with poor drainage, dig a small ditch to carry away excess water so the plants don't drown.

No matter where you plant, you may discover pest problems. Fortunately, several aromatics are effective bug deterrents. Make a tincture (see Chapter Two) of garlic, marigold, fennel, tomato leaves, catnip, basil, pennyroyal, bay, clove, eucalyptus, and golden seal. Sprinkle the tincture on your plants regularly, especially after rainfall, which washes off earlier applications. To combat more specific pests, refer to the following list and use the herb(s) similarly.

- Ants: mint, tansy, coffee grounds
- Aphids: fennel, garlic, marigold, mustard
- Japanese beetle: chive, tansy
- Leafhopper: geranium
- Mice: wormwood
- Mite: coriander
- Moles: narcissus
- Rabbit: marigold, onion
- Slug: rosemary, fennel

When harvesting, pick flower parts early in the morning before the sun dries out all the essential oils from the petals. Gather herbs when they mature, flowers when they first open, berries when they just ripen, and roots and barks in the fall. As you harvest, put each herb in separate, well-marked containers to avoid mix-ups later. This is especially important when making remedial products. Finally, process your herbs quickly. The fresher, the better! If you've harvested only one item for a specific preparation, use it shortly after. Leave yourself enough time for preserving after mass harvesting.

Buying Herbs

Not everyone has the space or time to grow their own herbs, so it's important to know where to buy the best herbal products and what to look for in a supplier. If you are shopping in person for fresh herbs, first smell the plant. Good aromatics will always have a distinct scent. Also, scrutinize the herbs' display area and look for signs of pests, mold, wilted leaves, or dull coloration. This indicates either a poor crop or poor management.

When buying dried herbs, your supermarket is likely not the best option. Check food cooperatives, health food stores, or organic mail order suppliers instead. Herbs stored in clear glass lose their flavor and medicinal quality far more readily than those in dark containers. If you're sure of their freshness but the container isn't the best, repackage your purchases at home and make sure the jars are sterilized and properly labeled. Frozen herbs generally last for six months, and dried herbs will last for a year.

Exploring suppliers independently opens a world of possibilities beyond what mainstream avenues offer. Do research before deciding on an herb supplier and consider purchasing from small local businesses. By shopping locally, you support your community and may even find herbs unique to your local landscape!

Preserving and Storing Herbs

If you've grown your own herbs or purchased a large quantity of fresh ones, you will likely want to preserve some for other times and applications. Each part of an herb is processed slightly differently. For example, stems, leaves, flowers, berries, and seeds can often be dried in bundles. Cut the stem about four inches down from the tip, tie about ten stems together, and hang upside down in a dark, aerated area. If you are specifically harvesting seeds, tie a paper bag around the bundle to gather any loose seeds as they dry.

Flower heads can also be cut from the stem and laid out to dry on a clean piece of screen. The parts easily come free of the stem for sorting when dry. Put each component into a brown glass jar with an airtight lid and label. Rose petals, parsley, chickweed, and similar herbs freeze well.

Underground portions of herbs (roots, rhizomes, and tubers) are best harvested after the aboveground portion of the plant withers. Clean them thoroughly with warm water and cut off any unwanted parts. Dice into small pieces or slices and spread these on paper towels in a warm (not hot) oven for two hours. Finally, move the roots into a spot where they remain open to the air but protected from pets and dirt until completely dried. Berries can be dried similarly, except they need about three hours in the oven. For evenness, turn the fruit occasionally and replace damp paper towels as needed.

Collect bark from outlying branches and remove any dirt, insects, or growths (like moss). Like roots, cut into smaller, usable segments and dry on a tray or piece of screen. You can also tap the same tree for sap in the spring by drilling a hole about ¼ inch in diameter. After gathering the sap, take care to fill the hole to prevent pest infestations and damage.

In all cases, a dehumidifier speeds the drying process considerably. You can microwave your herbs for no more than thirty-second intervals. Stop the microwave, check and turn the herbs, then repeat. Many herbs dry in under four minutes when microwaved.

Tools of the Trade

Like any artist, you will need to gather the proper implements to fashion your craft. A nice benefit of the herbal arts is that many of these tools are already in your home. I have included a list of constituents to make a serviceable herbal starter kit. This list incorporates everything needed to harvest, dry, and prepare the recipes in Chapter Two. Please make sure all utensils are sterilized prior to use.

Blender or Food Processor: Not a necessity, but these modern conveniences make some herbal beverages and foods easier to prepare. Food processors can also help produce consistently sized herb pieces to preserve. Be extra mindful in washing either of these after you're finished—the blades hide minute leftovers very easily.

Cheesecloth: Often found in the cleaning supplies aisle at the supermarket, cheesecloth is used to strain various preparations like teas and wines.

Compost Container: In line with the "waste not, want not" principle and to make your art earth-friendly, compost your unused ends, stems, and pieces with other biodegradable items. Save and use the compost each year to fertilize your garden or window boxes. Please make sure to check your local ordinances regarding compost containers outdoors since regulations vary by region.

Cutting Board: I do not recommend a wooden surface, as small bits of herbs and oils can get lodged in the surface while cutting. These small particles are very hard to see and clean out. Go with a stone, glass, ceramic, or hard plastic surface instead.

Funnel: Get several of these, each with a different diameter so they can fit in containers of various sizes.

Jars: Recycle these whenever possible, washing and sterilizing any you plan to reuse. Examine all your jars carefully for cracks or chips. Do *not* use any containers in either condition.

Dark glass is preferable for storing herbs. It keeps herbs fresh longer as light and heat damage potency. For herbal preparations like creams, any receptacle is fine but glass is best. Small jars that once held baby food, jelly, airplane liquor, maple syrup, cough syrup, and the like are perfect containers for gift-giving and storage. Some drugstores sell apothecary-style jars in many sizes at reasonable prices at the prescription counter. When you want something fancier, import stores often have a wide selection of glass bottles perfect for oils, creams, and vinegars. The average price on one to two-ounce jars is under $3.00 per jar.

Knives: Steel is best, but any sharp kitchen knife will do.

Labels: I cannot stress enough the importance of good, conscientious labeling. Depending on the size of your containers, mailing labels and file folder labels are two frugal choices. Each label should clearly indicate the date of the herb's harvest (or drying) or product's creation along with its contents.

Always use indelible marker on labels. This way, you can still identify its contents if a jar accidentally gets wet.

Lace or Netting: A finely woven lace can replace cheesecloth as a strainer. Lace or netting can be hung in an arid, dark area to dry herbs. (The advantage here is that most people have abundant ceiling space.) Finally, lace and netting can catch seeds from harvested plants if you carefully tie a small swatch around the head of a bundle.

Measuring Utensils: Get two sets of measuring cups and spoons, and, if possible, a good scale. Keep one set for consumable preparations and the other for nonedible products. This decreases the risk of potentially hazardous ingredients being mixed into foods.

Mortar and Pestle: While not necessary to your starter kit, this comes handy when macerating and grinding down herbs to a useful size and consistency.

Pots and Pans: Use glass, stainless steel, or enamel *only*. Aluminum taints your products' flavor and can also leach into them. Like your measuring utensils, keep one set of pots and pans strictly for nonedible preparations. Trust me—you will not want to cook food in any pan used for soap or perfume preparation!

Pruning scissors: Keep these handy to trim fresh herbs as needed or harvest the herbs at maturity. Clean and dry your scissors thoroughly after each use so that essential oils and plant matter don't dull the blades or mingle with the next herb cut.

Screening: Purchase clean rolls of fine screening at a hardware store. Use it to dry herbs or to cover drying herbs to keep pests and unwanted hands away. If you're feeling crafty, make two square wooden frames with screening and attach them at one side with a hinge. This will look like a book with screening as the front and back cover, and the wood as the binding. It will provide adequate air flow and protection while the herbs dry between the two screens.

Sealable Plastic Bags: Use these to freeze or store freshly harvested flower petals and herbs for later. Clean vegetable scraps can also be stored similarly and used for soup stock later.

Shelving: Like nature's abundance, herbal collections grow. I started with a few herbs that fit neatly on my spice rack; now, I have a whole wall dedicated to different components and products. I recommend stopping at secondhand stores and garage sales for several units like spice racks and bookshelves. Mount them in a well-ventilated, dimly lit area of your home.

Spatula: Try wooden spatulas over plastic so nothing gets wasted.

Spring Water: Especially nice for teas, tonics, and wines, spring water is free of the chemicals added to tap water.

String: I've used everything from twine to thread to successfully bundle and hang herbs.

Tea Ball or Other Sieves: It's nice to have a few different sizes of these to strain or steep herbs. They save time—especially in winemaking—by eliminating the need to filter out sediment.

Temperature Gauge and Timer: Some herbs and herbal products are sensitive to temperature. With practice, one can get a feel for timing and temperature without relying on a thermometer. Meanwhile, using one can reduce errors and prevent waste.

Vegetable or Nut Oils: Try not to skimp on these. Quality oils have a longer shelf life and more readily incorporate herbs. A cloudy oil indicates decay or rancidness and should be immediately disposed of.

Wax: Wax is handy to seal jars for transport and keeps air away from preparations for longer periods. Wax is also a constituent in some cream recipes found in Chapter Two.

Wooden Spoons: These are excellent for stirring soap and all types of cooking. They are a much better choice than plastic, which tends to retain odors.

The Hearth of the Matter

After assembling your starter kit, it's time to look at your workspace. A clean space is very important, especially when making remedials. Get rid of excess clutter so you have plenty of room, and then use a good disinfectant before you begin.

Gather all the necessary tools for the product beforehand and arrange them in the order they will be used. Likewise, place all the ingredients in the order they appear in the recipe. When you no longer need a tool or component, clean or store it away so you don't double up on any ingredient.

For the new herbalist, I recommend mastering *only* one product at a time before learning another. There are two reasons for this: first, one skill will almost always have applications elsewhere in the art. Secondly, this approach requires buying less ingredients and tools at the outset. When you're ready to try something new, review the recipe and purchase only what you need. In this manner, your art will grow and progress naturally with the fewest components possible. Hobbies do not have to be expensive to be fun and functional!

Stirring in Spirituality

Life seems to move at a warp speed, leaving little time to focus on the sacred and its significance to everyday reality. This is a terrible loss that may be rectified by creatively blending spirituality with mundane life. Herbalism is an art that does just that if you so wish.

Looking back at traditional herbals from the Renaissance, Nicholas Culpeper and John Gerald wrote that every plant had a predominant element and ruling astrological sign that impacted how an herb was applied. Earlier writings also reveal a wealth of folklore and superstition connected with herbs, many of which had strong mystical undertones (see Chapter Three). Additionally, numerous old recipes include magical instructions for harvesting or preparing herbs to enhance their effectiveness.

Some of the methods used by our ancestors to incorporate their spirituality include:

- ○ Harvesting ingredients or making the preparation during a waxing moon to encourage positive energy or a waning moon to banish illness.

○ Stirring a preparation clockwise, following the sun, to invoke blessings.

○ Using a symbolic number of ingredients, repetitions of an invocation or prayer, or treatment days (in the case of illness). The most common numbers are three, seven, and nine, with three representing the Holy Trinity, seven representing completion, and nine being three times three.

○ Choosing herbs based on color correspondences, such as a red flower to help with blood problems.

○ Using herbal associations from folklore to determine application. For example, a potion for devotion might include orange and lemon rind, which were believed to improve commitment (see Chapter Three).

These approaches work very well with a little creativity. While one wouldn't choose an herb only for its color, the final product could have a symbolic hue. For example, a calming cream could include lavender oil in a pale blue wax to engender peace, or an herbal tincture with a little bright yellow or red food coloring could increase energy.

To incorporate your religious beliefs and the associated positive energy into your art, consider the following ideas:

○ Playing personally significant and spiritually uplifting music while you work.

○ Burning specially prepared incense that conveys your prayers and wishes to the winds and the divine.

○ Lighting a candle to honor the divine presence in your kitchen.

○ Praying, reciting chants or mantras, or speaking invocations as you create your product. For example, a simple prayer could be:

Great Lord and Lady, Spirit of Creation, see the work of my hands and bless it for healing.

In place of healing, you may state your intention, whether that be love, prosperity, or peace.

o Chanting repeatedly, starting softly and slowly increasing in volume throughout the creation process to infuse your product with the spiritual energy raised from the chant. A chant might take this form:

I call the fire,
I call the wind,
I call Earth and water,
let magic begin!

o Timing your work with astrological influences appropriate to the goal of the finished product. Leverage Aries for matters of initiative, Taurus for vigor and fortitude, Gemini for skill and versatility, Cancer for emotions, Leo for power and strength, Virgo for prudence and detail, Libra for logic and balance, Scorpio for passion, Sagittarius for idealism and generosity, Capricorn for determination and organization, Aquarius for objectivity and communication, and Pisces for sensitivity and artistry.

To illustrate this with a vignette, imagine your friend has trouble with relationships. You could make them a love-drawing cream when the moon is in Cancer to balance their emotions or during Aquarius to improve their communication skills. Better still, add herbal oils that attract love to the cream, rose being one obvious choice.

It is important that the chosen actions or words have personal meaning. They don't have to make sense to anyone else, nor do they have to be fancy. The sacred powers care more about our intentions than about frills. So, relax and find a comfortable way to share your hearth, home, and herbal crafts with whatever vision of the divine you hold in your heart.

Creed of the Home Herbal Hobbyist

Creative vision is part of any art, so naturally, every herbalist approaches their art differently. Nonetheless, there are respectable guidelines, both old and new, for new herbalists. Consider this list as a pantry creed to which you can add your own inventiveness and insight in heaping quantities for effective and pleasing results:

- Whenever possible, do it yourself; you'll save money and know what's in your finished product. However, keep your time constraints in mind when beginning anything new. Some herbal preparations (like soap) cannot be rushed.
- Similarly, consider your budget. The higher the quality of the herbs, the higher the quality of your products will be. Regardless, many lovely and useful items can be made with spices found at home.
- When making remedial products, remember the rule "if one can cure, two can kill." Herbalism is not a substitute for professional medical attention, nor should a recipe's proportions exceed the recommendations without consulting an expert.
- Try to get organic components. This keeps excessive chemicals out of your body.
- Always work in reciprocity with the Earth; whatever you use, replace. This ensures that nature's supermarket stays stocked. Always make sure that what you buy is what you need. For example, a scented oil is one in which herbs have been steeped and is mild. An essential oil is a pure extraction and far more potent.
- Before picking or using any herbs, make certain of the plant's identity. Some plants have both edible and poisonous varieties. If you're not sure, don't use it.
- When gifting herbal products, always make the recipient aware of the ingredients to avoid possible allergic reactions.

- If possible or desired, find a meaningful way to incorporate your personal faith when you make your products. There is no dish, cream, tincture, or poultice that won't benefit from love mixed in as a little "soul food."
- Consider blending folklore and superstitions from your culture or family to personalize your products. For example, stir sunwise to encourage positive energy or sprinkle spilled salt over your shoulder to deter negativity. Such actions may seem a little out of place in our modern world, but they can have a profound impact on your attitude. When you feel positive and happy, your products bring out confidence and joy in others.
- If you have pets or children, consider childproof, shatter-resistant containers to house your herbs and preparations.
- Review different herbal books for ideas. One may have terrific soapmaking procedures, while another has neat ideas for perfumes. Every writer has specific areas of interest and expertise. By comparing sources, you're bound to come up with reliable and successful recipes.
- Remember to have fun and experiment a little. Mix and mingle to create something that is wholly yours. As long as you maintain the proper proportions, your ingenuity and ideals are expressed through herbalism's inherent inventiveness, while the practical side provides healthier, more natural living every day.

2

HERBAL ARTISTRY: SAMPLE RECIPES

"He that would know the reason of the operation of herbs must look up as high as the stars."
—Nicholas Culpeper

I vividly remember when I was first bitten by the herbalism bug. I met a woman selling her own soap at a historical re-creation event. The soap's aroma and texture were wonderful. When I asked how difficult it was to make, I got a surprising response: "Not at all!"

After scribbling down her instructions, I rushed home and immediately tried making soap. The experiment was a success, and I was hooked. What began as an iron pot of bubbling soap slowly expanded to homemade massage oils, perfumes for friends, incense, teas, and numerous other products.

However, finding recipes and adapting historical methods were not always as easy or successful as my first adventure. Consequently, this chapter supplies a helpmate to your herbal arts, one that I didn't have from the outset. You will find all kinds of recipes that incorporate your chosen herbs creatively and easily.

Unless Chapter Three (or another source) recommends different proportions, the proportions in this chapter are standard ratios. Some herbs, however, require different preparation times or proportions for safety reasons, so please read the instructions carefully. Remember that remedial recipes are not a substitute for sound medical care. The recipes appear in alphabetical order with illustrative combinations.

Air Freshener

Begin with one cup of re-melted candle ends and pieces. Add ten drops of essential oil or a finely powdered blend of aromatic herbs, not exceeding an eighth of a cup. Cool this mixture until it can be easily handled. Next, make a loop of wick about six inches long. Shape the wax decoratively around the wick, leaving about three inches outside of the wax. (I find a teardrop shape forms easily and looks pretty when completed.) Allow it to finish cooling, then decorate as you wish and hang in a sunny window to release its aroma. When the scent fades, use it as a candle!

Aftershave

Begin with ¼ cup rubbing alcohol, ¼ cup witch hazel tincture, and ½ cup cider vinegar. In a large jar, add the mixture to a blend of ⅓ cup mint, ⅓ cup calendula petals, and ⅓ cup sage. Other recommended herbs include rosemary, savory, lavender, lemon, and raspberry leaf.

Beer

Historical accounts of beer brewing date as far back as 6000 BCE, possibly earlier. Many civilizations, including those of Egypt, Greece, and Rome, valued it for enjoyment and as a foundational medicinal substance. Early beers were rarely without herbal additives, and even St. Hildegard, a twelfth-century Benedictine nun, used beer to heal the sick.

While there are numerous approaches, the brewing method here is chemical-free and uses tools readily found at home. It is based on a twelfth-century Germanic blend used as a digestive aid and tonic.

Heat four quarts of hot water with a two-inch piece of minced ginger root, a pinch of rosemary and fennel, one peeled orange, one pound of malt, and one and a half cups of honey or sugar. Steep until lukewarm. Next, add a quarter ounce of suspended beer yeast to the mixture. Strain after twelve hours. This beer can be consumed within five days with a shelf life of about three to four months.

Substitute other herbs or increase the proportions to personalize the flavor. For a fruity beer, replace a third of the water with fruit juice.

Bath Oils and Infusions

Add ten drops of essential oil to your bathwater to release pleasant aromas. Change the oils to address specific skin problems or according to their aromatherapy applications.

Alternatively, bundle fresh herbs in a swatch of cheesecloth and let them float in the hot water for about five minutes before soaking. You can add loose herbs, but these tend to stop up pipes. To attract new love or improve relations, add roses, comfrey root, rosemary, carnations, lavender, fennel, thyme, mint, marjoram, basil, vervain, or lovage to your bath. For improved energy, try ginger and marigold petals. To relieve tension, use jasmine, lemon balm, and violet. To improve the skin, add dandelion, orange peel, and blackberry leaves.

Bath Salts

Begin with a base of Epsom salt, readily available at most drugstores, or sea salt. Add about twenty-five drops of essential oil(s) to one cup of salt. I also enjoy including finely diced dried herbs like lavender, citrus rinds, and roses. Add about five tablespoons of this to your tub water and store the remainder in an airtight container. *Warning:* Too much Epsom salt can irritate your skin, so make sure your tub is full!

This recipe also works for scented salts, especially when blended with oils known for their therapeutic aromas like rosemary.

Beads

These are made from flower petals, most commonly roses. Begin with a full quart pan of petals harvested early in the morning. If you do not have enough flower petals from a single day's harvest, freeze them until you accumulate enough.

Purée the flower petals in a blender with just enough water to cover them. Pour the mixture in a seasoned iron pot and simmer. Repeat this procedure daily for two weeks until the petals thicken into a paste-like texture. At this point, you can fashion beads and add matching essential oils to improve the finished aroma.

Mold the beads into balls twice the desired size. They will shrink as they dry. Use a good needle to create holes for stringing, turning the beads daily so they don't stick and the holes stay evenly formed. As an easy alternative, shape the beads around florist's wire hung across a small area, allowing you to easily spin the beads as they dry. The beads dry in approximately fourteen to twenty days and can be stored indefinitely.

Butter

The typical ratio of herb to butter, depending on how spicy you like things, is one tablespoon finely chopped herb to half cup of softened butter. Store in your refrigerator for one month or freeze for up to three months. Try combining mint and dill, orange and lemon rind, or basil with garlic and chives.

Candied Fruit Rinds

Besides drying and grinding fruit rinds, our ancestors frugally candied them for long-term storage, with recipes dating beyond the Middle Ages in France and England. To try this yourself, begin by scraping all the pith (the white matter) out of the peel. Soak the rinds in a mixture of spring water and two teaspoons of rose water for nine days, changing the water daily. Next, put the slices in a pot of fresh water, bringing them to a low rolling boil for one hour. Remove and dry.

On the next day, return the rinds to a pan and add enough honey to cover them. Bring to a boil and regularly skim the honey. When the honey candies (creating a ball in cool water), remove the rinds and place them on a nonstick surface such as wax paper. Sprinkle with a little ginger, cinnamon, vanilla sugar, or other traditional baking spices.

Cover with a loosely woven cloth for thirty days or until the rinds completely harden and dry. To dry them more quickly, place them in a warm oven. Once dry, the rinds last nearly forever, making an excellent breath mint or healthy snack.

Candles
Save candle ends and pieces or buy some beeswax at a hobby store. You can also save milk cartons or disposable cups from fast-food restaurants to use as molds.

Melt the wax over a low flame and add finely powdered herbs, essential oils, or a combination of both. Cool briefly before molding or your containers will melt. To loosen the candle from the mold, dip the container in a bath of hot water quickly and then cut it neatly away.

Carpet Freshener
Add one cup of finely ground herbs and ten drops of matching essential oils to six cups of baking soda. Mix thoroughly and store in an airtight container. Sprinkle on rugs a few minutes before vacuuming.

Cheese
Herbed cheeses may be made with cream cheese or any other solid cheese. For cream cheese, begin with one cup of the cheese and add two to three teaspoons of finely chopped herb. Mix thoroughly in a blender, then keep chilled until use. This blend is particularly tasty on bagels and raw vegetables.

Alternatively, take six ounces of grated cheese, four tablespoons of cream, and two to three tablespoons of powdered herb. Mix in a double boiler until the grated cheese melts and the herbs are well incorporated. Cool and refrigerate until serving. Try this blend as part of hot fondue.

Cleansers
Salt, baking soda, and sorrel leaves act as effective cleansers for pots, pans, floors, and countertops. Add essential oils to the salt or baking soda for a pleasant aroma. Note that salt should not be used on any surface prone to scratching.

Cleansing Bundles
Begin with eight-inch cuttings of herbs still on the stalk (sage, lavender, and lemongrass are good choices). Gather a one-and-a-half-inch bundle tightly and bind it firmly at the top using cotton string, wrapping it around multiple times. Next, hold the bundle firmly together (this needs to be very dense) and take sixteen inches of string, crisscrossing it down the length of the bundle at quarter-inch intervals and knotting it at each interval. Finally, tie off at the bottom.

Burn this instead of incense to deter nasty odors and lift the energy in a home. After use, douse the lit end with cold water and hang up to dry.

Coffee
Some herbs are used as coffee substitutes, including ground dried dandelion root. However, most people add herbs to coffee while brewing for improved aroma or a gourmet appeal. One to two teaspoons of herb are sufficient for a ten to twelve cup pot of coffee. Good choices include nutmeg and cinnamon. In the West Indies, vanilla beans are steeped in coffee, while cardamom seeds are added in the Arabian Peninsula, and roast chicory is a favorite in Europe.

Compresses

A compress is nothing more than a cloth soaked with an herbal infusion or tincture. Compresses may be applied warm or cold depending on the skin condition. Lay it on the skin, re-soaking and applying frequently for best results.

Creams

For making a cream, use a ratio of one part dried herb to three parts oil and five parts wax. Place these ingredients in a pan over low heat—or better yet in a double boiler—and simmer for two to three hours. Strain out the herbs using cheesecloth, then beat the mixture until it cools completely.

Cocoa butter or coconut oil may replace any portion of wax to condition the skin if you wish. Also, consider adding suitable essential oils to increase aroma and improve shelf life. About five drops of essential oil in a half-ounce container works well.

Another alternative is adding lanolin to the mixture. The proportions for this preparation are a quarter ounce of wax, two ounces of almond oil, a half-ounce of lanolin, and a half-ounce of herbal water. Prepare as before, choosing your herb(s) according to your skin's needs. For example, use wintergreen, sage, lemon, or bay as an astringent. Lavender and geranium mixed together make a toning cream, and bay with thyme or myrrh is good as an antiseptic cream.

Decoctions

Decoctions are a concentrated infusion, usually ingested in small quantities. Bark, roots, rhizomes, and berries are frequently simmered to extract the useful constituents, each lending itself readily to the decoction form. Prepare as you would an infusion but steep the herbs instead for at least eight hours. Next, strain out the herbs and simmer the liquid until it reduces by one-third (about twenty-five minutes).

Store in the refrigerator for no more than two days. To extend the shelf life, add two tablespoons brandy to half cup of liquid. Average dosage is two to three teaspoons, three times daily.

Deodorant

Add fifteen drops of an essential oil to two cups of spring water. Add to a pump spray and shake well before each use. To allay body odor, good choices include pine, cedar, sage, and lemon.

Dyes

Many herbs make an excellent base for dying fabric. For best results, use fully-bloomed flowers, ripened berries, bark and leaves taken in spring, and roots from fall harvests. In all cases, fresh herbs provide richer color than dried herbs.

To adhere to the fabric, herbs need a chemical enhancer, the most common being alum, chrome, tin, and iron. Use the following proportions in the herb bath:

- ½ lb pre-washed fabric
- 2 gallons water
- ½–¾ lb herbs, depending on how dark you want the dye
- 2 oz alum with ½ oz cream of tartar, or ¼ oz chrome with ½ oz cream of tartar, or ¼ oz tin and ¼ oz cream of tartar

The herb chosen depends on the desired color. Yarrow is suitable for black, elder for blue, fennel or geranium for brown, goldenrod for gold, poplar for gray, marjoram for green, sunflower for orange, bloodroot for pink, blackberries for purple, dandelion for red, and chamomile for yellow. These are just a few examples of herbs that produce dye colors. Additional options are discussed in Chapter Three.

Simmer ingredients until they reach a low boil, then reduce the heat. Add fabric and steep for at least one hour (or longer for darker hues). Stir regularly to ensure even dyeing. Rinse the fabric and hang to dry. Keep in mind that dyeing might leave a lingering scent in the pot, so refrain from using it for cooking.

Elixirs

Add a half cup of water to one cup of tincture. The *Elixir of Life,* or *aqua vitae,* was a popular elixir during the Middle Ages that promised a long life and good health. The elixir was comprised of tinctures from bay, cardamom, angelica, lemon, fennel, licorice, clove, chamomile, anise, ginger, nutmeg, cinnamon, mace, and sage, formulated in a base of brandy. Water and honey were added for a pleasant flavor, though honey may also have been included due to its strong mystical associations with well-being, as it was considered sacred to numerous deities, including Artemis (Greece), Min (Egypt), and Kama (India).

Facials

Herbal facials effectively open and cleanse the pores. The simplest form of a facial is prepared like an inhalant. Mix a quart of boiling water with a quarter cup of any or all of the following in a bowl: rosemary, fennel, chamomile, comfrey, clover, lemon, rose, lavender, and pansy. Steam your face using a towel to hold in the heat and moisture. Rinse with herb water or vinegar. For oily skin, rinse with a blend of lemon juice and rose water; for dry skin, try an orange and mint wash.

Fomentations

Take a clean piece of woven cloth or gauze and dip in a warm decoction or infusion. Wring out the cloth and apply to the afflicted area.

Hair Conditioner

Begin with an ounce of almond oil. Add two drops each of rosemary and lavender oil plus five drops of any of the following: rosemary or sage for dark hair, calendula for light hair, comfrey for dry hair, or thyme or nettle for oily hair and dandruff. Massage this mixture into your scalp, leaving in place for fifteen minutes before shampooing and rinsing.

Alternatively, add five to seven drops of lavender oil to a base of half an ounce of rosemary oil. Add five drops of vanilla or sage for dark hair, five drops of lemon or chamomile for blond hair, or five drops of saffron for red hair. Apply the mixture to a hairbrush or comb and distribute evenly through your hair.

Hair Rinse

Make your hair rinse as you would any herbal water, except choose the herbs according to hair color and requirements (sage or rosemary for brown hair or chamomile for light hair). Those with dandruff will benefit from a sage and nettle rinse. *Hint:* Warm the rinse in a microwave gently before use.

Ice Cream

Warm one cup of cream with one and a half cups of milk and two to three teaspoons of herb. Bring close to a boil, then remove from heat and cover, allowing the blend to sit undisturbed for an hour before straining. Meanwhile, beat three egg yolks until fluffy. Set aside as you rewarm the cream mixture. Whisk a little of the hot cream into the eggs, then pour everything back into the pan to cook until it reaches a custard consistency. Cool, then freeze halfway, beating again thoroughly until smooth. If you wish, add finely diced fruit. Serve with a garnish of fresh herbs.

Incense

To make incense cones, begin with a base of four teaspoons of sandalwood powder, one teaspoon of gum arabic, and twenty teaspoons of any dried herbs. Mix no more than three dried herbs into any one scent for best results. In another bowl, blend a quarter cup of saltpeter with a quarter cup of water. Slowly add this liquid into the dry mixture until it reaches a doughy consistency. Shape the incense into cones and set them upright in a sunny area for three days to dry before storing.

For incense requiring self-lighting charcoal, begin by adding finely powdered herbs to an aromatic wood base. Proportions vary based on the herbs' potency and the desired final aroma, so experiment a bit here. Once satisfied, sprinkle one to two pinches on hot charcoal (or an outdoor fire to repel bugs), adding more as desired. If you add essential oils to the wood powder, ensure they are thoroughly mixed and allowed to dry before use.

Infusions

Infusions are easily preparable and have a tea-like quality that can be consumed hot or cold. The average recommended measurement is two teaspoons of fresh herb or one teaspoon of dried herb steeped in one cup of water. Steep dried roots and barks for eight hours, leaves for about three hours, flowers for one hour, and seeds for thirty minutes. To avoid straining, use a tea ball or small swatch of cheesecloth to house the herbs.

For remedial purposes, most infusions are taken two to four times daily. Store the excess in your refrigerator for no more than thirty-six hours. Add a dab of honey to infusions with unpalatable flavors, like valerian or eucalyptus.

Inhalations, Steams

In a bowl, combine five to ten drops of essential oil, such as eucalyptus, bayberry, and pine, with one liter of boiled water. Cover your head with a towel, close your eyes, and inhale the steam until the mixture cools. If at any time you feel dizzy or overheated, stop immediately.

Steams work similarly. Add four tablespoons of herbs suited to your skin to one quart of boiling water. For dry skin, consider elder or rose; for oily skin, add a slice of lemon and a slice of grapefruit. Since steam opens the pores, you may wish to enjoy a facial mask or herbal wash afterward.

Laundry Freshener

Combine one teaspoon of powdered orange or lemon rind with two to three drops of your preferred aromatic oil in one cup of baking soda. Mix thoroughly, then add one teaspoon of the mixture during the rinse cycle.

Liniment

A liniment is a tincture applied externally for muscle and ligament trauma. When you need one quickly, add essential oil to alcohol and shake well. I frequently use part alcohol and part oil for decocting liniment. This mixture is less likely to irritate sensitive skin and can be rubbed in smoothly like a massage oil. Recommended herbs for effective, stimulating rubs include cinnamon, wintergreen, cayenne (caution!), bayberry, eucalyptus, and camphor.

Liqueurs

Liqueurs may be flavored with spices, fruits, or a combination of both, and are generally served before dinner to improve appetite or after dinner to aid digestion. Begin with a quart of any distilled beverage, adding one to two pounds of fruit or a quarter cup of chosen herbs (or a combination of both) and half to two-thirds cup of honey (or sugar).

Use a small amount of distilled beverage to melt the honey for incorporation, then add the ingredients to a sealed bottle. Shake daily for at least two to three weeks before straining. Allow the liqueur to age if you can resist temptation! Good combinations include blackberries with ginger in brandy; apricots with vanilla in vodka; and oranges, cinnamon, and strawberries in rum.

Historically, physicians and homemakers alike often made remedial liqueurs, frequently with brandy as a base to cover the flavor of less agreeable ingredients. For colds and flu, clove, ginger, cinnamon, peppermint, orange, and sage were added with honey. For an overall tonic, a blend of bay, cardamom, angelica, fennel, lemon rind, chamomile, anise, nutmeg, and mace might be used. Enhance the flavor of these beverages with fruit juice.

Massage Oils

For fast, effective massage oils, combine one tablespoon of almond oil with five to ten drops of the desired aromatic oil(s). This can be heated briefly in the microwave before applying (see also *Oils*).

Meads

Meads are honey wines and have a long history as offerings to divine beings and as medicine. This association is in part attributed to honey, renowned for its heavenly sweetness and its purported mystical and magical qualities, like encouraging the muse!

A basic mead is not difficult to prepare, consisting of honey, water, a slice of citrus, and yeast. Nearly any herb or combination of herbs can be added to this base during the cooking process for variety, flavor, or to enhance magical purpose.

Add two and a half pounds of honey to one gallon of warm water. Bring to a low rolling boil, skimming away any scum that rises from the honey over the next hour. Add the fruits and herbs during the last twenty minutes of heating; the average ratio is sixteen to twenty-five teaspoons of herbs or fruits to one gallon of liquid depending on how strong you want the flavor. Remove from the flame and cool down to lukewarm. Meanwhile, combine a quarter cup of warm water with one tablespoon wine or mead yeast in a separate container and let sit.

When the honey-water is cool, pour in the yeast mixture. Place a clean kitchen towel over the entire pot and let stand for three days. Strain and pour into glass jugs and loosely cork the jugs or place a balloon over the mouth of the bottles with a rubber band. This releases the pressure from fermentation safely. Do not cork tightly; the bottles might explode from the pressure.

After about four weeks, cork the bottles more securely or replace the balloon with a screw top. Open the bottle slightly every two to three days to relieve excess pressure (especially in warmer climates).

After eight weeks, I suggest racking the mead. Pour or siphon off the clear liquid in the top three-quarters of the bottle into smaller containers. Let the mead age another two to four months undisturbed in a cool, dark area, then enjoy!

If you cannot find wine or mead yeast, bread yeast works but leaves an odd flavor. Additionally, do *not* use what most people call brewer's yeast. This is inactive, and your mead will not ferment.

Milk

Herbal milks are often used in beauty treatments. Begin by steeping four tablespoons of herb in one cup of whole milk overnight and keep refrigerated. Choose the herbs according to your skin type: chamomile for dry skin, and lavender or mint for oily skin. Strain and keep cold. Wash your face with warm water, then apply the mixture with a cotton ball and rinse.

As a twist to your everyday glass of milk, try sprinkling a little cinnamon, nutmeg, or ginger. This is even tastier in warm milk or eggnog.

Moisturizers

The easiest way to make moisturizer is with a base of honey. For small quantities, mix a quarter cup of honey with a half cup of any preferred herb water. Dab this on areas prone to dryness as needed.

Mouthwash

Begin with an infusion or a decoction of an antiseptic herb, such as myrrh and licorice, and an herb for flavoring, such as mint, and allow the mixture to cool before using. Use in half-cup portions.

Oils

Oils can be made in three different ways. The easiest method starts with one cup of good quality oil, like olive or almond oil, adding a few drops of essential oil until the aroma is pleasing. Please take care not to exceed any recommended amounts if consuming the oil or placing it on your skin. Some essential oils are not digestible, and others are volatile in larger concentrations.

The second method begins with one part dried herb or two parts fresh herb to three parts of a good quality oil. Put this in a double boiler, cover, and simmer for about two and a half hours. Allow the mixture to cool, then strain off the oil through a cheesecloth into a suitable container. These oils last for about six months if kept in a cool, dark area.

The third method has the same proportions as the second method, except the herb(s) and oil are added to a clear glass jar. Leave covered under a sunlit window, shaking the mixture daily for two weeks, then strain. If the oil is for aromatic purposes, reuse the base oil and add more herbs until you reach the desired concentration. While more time consuming, this is a preferred method of oil making, as some herbs are very sensitive to direct heating (rose is a good example). For culinary oils, try basil, garlic, oregano, and thyme based in olive oil; ginger and lemon verbena in safflower oil; and tarragon and celery seed in peanut oil. Use in sauces or as a marinade for sautéing. If your oil becomes cloudy or develops an unusual odor, throw it out.

Ointments

The base for an ointment varies. Petroleum jelly or wax works effectively, as does coconut oil and cocoa butter, depending on the final application method. Alternatively, mix the bases to create a blend specifically suited to your skin's needs.

The average ratio for an ointment is one part dry herb or one and a half parts fresh herb to five parts base. Place the herb into the base and warm it on the stove for one and a half hours. Strain and pour into jars with airtight lids. Add a little olive oil or aloe for a smoother ointment that spreads easily and resembles a cream.

For remedial purposes, ointments are applied three times daily. They have a very long shelf life.

Plasters

Bruise the herb by gently pressing on it with the flat of a spoon
or pound it lightly with a food mallet. Dampen the bruised
herb with boiling water. Place the mixture between two pieces
of woven cloth and apply to the afflicted area. A well-known
example for chest congestion is made from mustard seed.

Pomanders

Herald Newman's *Illustrated Dictionary of Jewelry* defines a
pomander as "highly scented spices and perfumes made into
a ball and carried in Medieval times to counteract offensive odors
and also to protect against infection." Queen Elizabeth I's favorite
pomander incorporated musk, ambergris, benzoin, and rose
water. Today, pomanders are used as bug repellents, aromatics, or
stench controllers, depending on the chosen herbs. For example,
pennyroyal and fennel work well to steer away insects.

To make a pomander, take equal portions of herbs or dried
flower petals with benzoin and just enough water to make a paste.
Add a few drops of essential oil to improve the effectiveness
and a few drops of beeswax if the mixture doesn't hold its
shape well. Roll everything in a ball and wrap it in one layer
of cheesecloth to dry. Place in any area where strong odors
persist or bugs hide.

Alternatively, begin with an orange, lemon, or lime. Carefully
push whole cloves into the fruit's skin until it is completely
covered. If the cloves break, poke holes in the fruit with a needle
or toothpick before inserting. Dust the clove-covered fruit with
a mixture of orris root, cinnamon, and ginger powder, then store
it in a dark, dry area for a month. Finally, hang with decorative
ribbon, add to a potpourri basket, or use in a drawer. Refresh
with a few drops of essential oil as needed.

Potpourri

Potpourri consists of larger pieces of aromatic herbs, including
well-dried barks, berries, petals, leaves, and peels. Consider
not only the aroma of each herb, but also how their colors

blend in a mixture. Once you achieve a pleasing blend, add a tablespoon of orris root powder per quart of herbs and several drops of your preferred essential oil. Thoroughly mix everything together in a ceramic or glass bowl before transferring it to a decorative receptacle. If the scent begins to fade, you may add more essential oil at any time. Leaving the basket or bundle in sunlight releases the aroma readily, but you will also have to refresh it more frequently.

For a forest-inspired blend, use herbs like marjoram, pine needles, sandalwood chips, thyme, and vetiver oil. For a cozy kitchen, combine allspice berries, cinnamon sticks, cloves, dried ginger, nutmeg, and vanilla oil.

Poultices

A poultice consists of fresh or dried herbs applied directly to the skin. To prepare, place enough bruised herbs to cover the affected area in a pot and simmer with water or herbal tincture for two minutes to warm and activate the useful oils. Apply to the skin with gauze or cotton to hold it in place. Leave the poultice in place for at least one hour and replace as needed. To relieve muscle strain, try St. John's wort. For boils, apply calendula mixed with myrrh tincture.

An alternative is a clay poultice. Begin with a quarter cup of cosmetic clay as a base. Add a quarter cup of water and two drops of the desired oil, then mix so the clay spreads easily. This mixture is useful for soothing discomfort caused by insect stings or other skin irritations.

Powders

Various herbs can serve as a base for body powder, including arrowroot, unscented talc, cornstarch, baking soda, and ground soapstone. I prefer the ground soapstone for its silky texture and noncarcinogenic quality, but grinding is very time-consuming.

Add twenty-five drops of essential oil and a half cup of finely diced herb to one cup of base powder. Store in an airtight container and shake regularly for two weeks. Sift before using.

Sachets and Pillows

Sachets can be made in any size. To make your life easier, find nice cloth napkins at yard sales and wrap crumbled herbs in the center. Simply tie with ribbon, and maybe add some dried flowers, then you're done! Smaller sachets can be placed among clothing to keep items smelling fresh and to deter insects; large ones are decorative and functional pillows for every area of the home, from the living room couch to your pet's bed.

To bring sweet dreams, begin with two six-inch pieces of fabric sewn on three sides. Stuff with pine needles (balsam is an excellent choice), hops, lavender, and a hint of lemon rind, then secure the final side. When the aroma fades, open it up and add a few drops of essential oil. For animals suffering from fleas, make a pillow for their beds with strong aromatics like fennel, mint, and lemon balm. Just be careful not to use any herbs that are toxic to them!

Salves

Add one tablespoon of beeswax to one ounce of herbal oil and melt over a low flame. Remove from heat and cool. As with ointments, coconut oil, cocoa butter, or vitamin E oil may be added as a skin conditioner. If the salve is firm to the touch but still melts on the skin when applied, then the proportions were correct.

Savory Salts

Those who need to monitor salt intake will find herbalism a refreshing and tasty ally. Beef benefits from a blend of pepper, rosemary, grated orange, garlic, dried onion, or marjoram. On poultry, mix and match ginger with sage, thyme, tarragon, and basil. Add zest to fish with dill, mustard, celery seeds, pepper, and lemon peel. For vegetables, sprinkle on dill, bay, chives, and basil.

Scrubs and Facial Masks

Begin with two cups of rolled oats, finely ground almonds, or a combination of both. Mix in six tablespoons of dried flowers and blend them. Once the consistency is even, slowly add rose water to create a paste. Rub this into your skin after soaking your pores with warm water. Rinse.

If your skin tends toward the dry side, try rose petals and a little almond oil in the blend. For oily skin use peppermint. Either of these compounds can become the foundation for a face mask by mixing them in equal proportions with almond oil, honey, and yogurt. Apply liberally, leave on for fifteen minutes, and then rinse thoroughly with warm water.

Smelling Salts

These are easy to make and last forever. Take a half cup of sea salt or Epsom salt and add a few drops of any uplifting herbs like rosemary or lavender. Take care to make the aroma pleasant and not overwhelming. Hold this mixture about three inches beneath your nose. When you feel woozy, let the aroma refresh you.

Soaps

Making soap at home is easier than expected. Begin with eight cups of liquid vegetable oil in a large non-aluminum pot. I use ironware; enamel is another good choice. In a ceramic dish, blend three cups of water with one cup of pure lye and stir. Do this in a well-ventilated area, as the lye fumes are very harsh.

Allow the lye mixture to cool down to lukewarm. Meanwhile, heat the vegetable oil to a similar temperature. Remove the oil from the heat and slowly stir in the cooled lye until the oil takes on a creamy color and consistency. Once the lye is incorporated, sprinkle in any finely powdered herbs or herbal oils for aroma or skin treatment. Essential oils should not exceed two percent of volume, and fillers should not exceed fifteen percent of volume.

Oatmeal powder with finely ground hops is an excellent cleansing blend, whereas soap with powdered kitchen spices is more for pleasure. To condition the skin, add an eighth cup of coconut oil, cocoa butter, lanolin, or aloe. Pour the entire mixture into a nine inch by six inch by two inch wooden box (old wine boxes work very well) lined with damp linen. If the soap is scented, dot a few drops of essential oil evenly over the damp linen to improve the soap's aroma.

Over the top of the box, place a piece of plywood, cardboard, or a heavy cloth to retain the heat. Leave the soap to solidify for twenty-four to thirty-six hours before checking it. If the soap is solid, you can cut it into bar shapes, but do not remove the bars from the container for another fourteen days.

If your soap separates, reclaim it by cutting up any solid parts into your pan and pouring in the residual liquid. Add four pints of water and warm over a low heat. Slowly increase the temperature until the mix boils and becomes ropy. At that point, you can re-pour the soap into the mold and age. This yields a very dense soap. When you remove the bars from the box, wrap the bars in scrap fabric or paper for storage. There is no maximum shelf life for soap; in fact, the longer it ages, the better it gets! Note, however, that homemade soaps do not lather like commercial brands because they lack chemicals. If you prefer more suds, add two tablespoons of borax to the solution while cooling. Nonetheless, the basic recipe cleans just fine and lasts far longer than commercial brands. Some suggested herbal blends include frankincense and myrrh powder for Yule, or strawberry and grapefruit as a refreshing summer soap.

For a liquid soap to use in the kitchen or bath, simply take your bars and cut up a half pound of them, adding a half gallon of water. Boil this for fifteen minutes, then cool. Keep soap in an airtight container or it will dry out.

Soda Pop

During the Victorian era, soda pop was dispensed by the druggist! Now, we can make our own. For every cup of sparkling water or club soda, add one to two teaspoons of herbal extract to taste along with your preferred sweetener. For a tasty summer treat, blend at high speed in a blender with crushed ice and fresh fruit until well-incorporated.

Sorbet

Begin by infusing one and a half pints of water or fruit juice with chosen herbs until it has a heady scent. Strain, then stir in a quarter cup of sugar (or less if using fruit juice as a base). Warm the mixture without boiling until the sugar dissolves, then transfer it to the freezer until it forms a slushy consistency. In the meantime, beat an egg white until fluffy, then whisk into the slushy mixture and freeze until served.

Sugar

To flavor or scent sugar for baking, add dried herb to the sugar jar. Vanilla bean with a few pieces of lemon or orange rind make a lovely blend for many cakes, pies, and other desserts.

Syrup

Syrups are created from a base of sugar or honey. They may be used in numerous preparations, including flavoring cordials, basting meats, and soothing a sore throat. Add one cup of herbal infusion or decoction to one cup of honey or sugar. Heat slowly until the honey or sugar dissolves and the mixture thickens. Cool, then store in glass jars using cork stoppers. Sometimes the syrup ferments, so using some other form of stopper might cause explosions.

Syrups may be prepared as a baste with whole and dry herbs instead of an infusion. For a poultry glaze, combine two cloves of garlic, one slice of lemon and orange, a slice of bruised ginger, and a pinch of rosemary with one cup of warm honey. Allow to age for a few weeks before use. When strained, this variation is also an effective cough syrup.

For baking syrups, flower mixtures make unique and flavorful alternatives, like rose syrup on vanilla ice cream. The shelf life for syrup is about six months. For remedial purposes, the recommended dosage is one teaspoon taken three times daily. Do not feed honey to children younger than one year old.

An alternative recipe for syrup takes one ounce of herb boiled in twenty ounces of water for twenty minutes in a closed container. Strain this and add one ounce of glycerin before bottling.

Tea

Take one to two teaspoons of dried herb to one cup of water—unless a remedial recipe calls for different proportions—then cover and steep for twenty minutes before consuming.

Tinctures

The word *tincture* refers to the fact that, once prepared, these liquids have a tint of color to them. Tinctures are alcohol-based, predominantly rum or vodka. Place one cup of herbs in five cups of alcohol. Close the jar tightly (remembering to label it) and shake the mixture every couple of days for one month. After straining, store in an airtight container and place in the refrigerator or another cool area.

For remedial purposes, take one teaspoon twice daily. If the flavor is too strong, mix the tincture with fruit juice. Tinctures may be stored in a cool, dark area for two to three years.

Toothpaste

Combine a quarter cup of baking soda with four teaspoons of salt, two teaspoons of lavender tincture, and one drop each of clove, mint, and vanilla. Stir and add water if necessary to create a pasty texture. Store in an airtight container.

Vinegar

Choose a base vinegar that brings out the flavor of the desired herbs. Begin with three to four sprigs or leaves of fresh herb to one cup of warmed vinegar. Let this sit until cool, then taste. For a stronger taste, add more herbs and repeat the process.

Tasty combinations for flavored vinegars include rosemary with orange in white vinegar; dill, garlic, and oregano in wine vinegar; and chive, savory, and parsley in cider vinegar. Vinegars are great on salads and as marinades and last for about one year. Like oils, discard if they begin to look cloudy.

Wash

Use a half ounce of herb to two pints of water for a mild infusion that may be applied externally.

Waters

Herb waters are like teas, but used for beauty treatments, such as facial rinses and finger bowls. Floral waters require approximately six cups of petals to one quart of water in order to create a rich aroma. Other spices integrate more easily and require less material than petals. For a tea, double the proportions. If it is not fragrant enough, strain and rewarm the original water with fresh herb.

Wine

For a simple remedial wine, steep a handful of herbs in a prepared wine base for four to six weeks, and then strain. If the herbs or the top of the wine look moldy, discard it. Otherwise, the resulting tonic lasts for about three months. Drink one glass daily for remedial purposes.

To make herbal wines from scratch, begin with one gallon of water in a non-aluminum pot and add two to three pounds of sugar (more if you like sweet wines). Bring to a low rolling boil with two to four slices of any citrus fruit and twelve bags of herbal tea (this eliminates the need for straining later). Follow the same steps used for making mead (see pages 35-36), including adding yeast, straining, storage, and aging. You may also add fruit juices with the herbs for fuller-flavored wines. Enjoyable combinations include orange bergamot with ginger, berries with cinnamon, and almond or mint with vanilla.

Herbal Theme Baskets

Besides taking better care of our health and our homes, the herbal arts offer an opportunity to make thoughtful, unique gifts for friends and loved ones. Any of the recipes in this chapter could be gifted in a decorative container. For example, you could make a unique herbed vinegar, leaving in the whole herbs, and put it in a specially purchased glass bottle with a cork, ribbon, and a few dried flowers.

An herbal themed basket is a particularly enjoyable and much-appreciated gift. Consider the occasion or the need, then make an entire cache of goodies to deliver with a smile. For a sick friend, make teas, an herb pillow, some aromatherapy bath salts, and old-fashioned chicken soup. For a friend feeling sad, put together items with uplifting aromas.

Through these baskets, your art becomes a blessing to everyone in and around your life. The world can always use a little extra thoughtfulness and kindness.

3

HERB MULTIPEDIA

"The book of Nature is that which the physician must read; and to do so he must walk over the leaves."
—Paracelsus

Agrimony
Agrimonia eupatoria

Folk Names: Church steeples, sticklewort, cocklebur
History: The species name originated with a 63 BCE Turkish king, Mithridates Eupator, who was very wise in the use of this herb and its related lore. Pliny regarded it as an herb of princely authority.
Folklore, Superstition, Magic: In medieval England, agrimony was used in potions to induce magical sleep.
Medicinal: As a mildly apricot-flavored tea, agrimony is good for the liver and sore throats. The aerial parts work effectively against children's diarrhea. Take infusions three times daily.

Culinary, Crafts: Agrimony may be used in flavoring beer. Use six ounces of agrimony per barrel. When mixed with alum, agrimony can be used as a homemade dye in gold or yellow.

Gardening, Habitat: Native to Europe, agrimony prefers marshy regions and fares well in most northern temperate zones.

Other: In the language of flowers, agrimony represents gratitude.

Alder
Alnus glutinosa

Folk Names: Owler

History: Alder was the predominant wood used in building Venice.

Folklore, Superstition, Magic: Across different cultures, alder was believed to house evil spirits because of the bloodlike coloring of its sap. In the Celtic tree alphabet, alder represents the letter "F." Homer alludes to the alder as a tree of resurrection in the *Odyssey*.

Medicinal: Wooster Beech, a healer of the eighteenth century, recommended alder bark decoctions as a blood cleanser. In modern times, the bark and leaves are effective mild astringents, best used in mouthwashes to ease bleeding gums or applied to mild cuts, scrapes, and itchy bug bites.

Culinary, Crafts: Extract crimson dye from alder bark, green dye from the leaves, and brown or black from the twigs. The green dye is said to have been used in Robin Hood's and fairies' clothing.

Gardening, Habitat: A native tree to Europe, Asia, and North Africa, alder grows best in damp regions and near water sources. For best results, gather alder bark in the spring.

Other: When your feet ache, place alder leaves in your shoes. Apply warm leaves to the skin to ease discomfort from engorgement while nursing. However, alder should not be used during pregnancy as it contracts mucous membranes.

Alfalfa
Medicago sativa

Folk Names: Lucerne, medick

History: By 2939 BCE, the Chinese had already incorporated alfalfa as a vegetable. The Spanish monks in Mexico often surrounded their missions with alfalfa for use in making teas and remedial blends.

Folklore, Superstition, Magic: A house in which alfalfa grows will never want; it is an herb of providence.

Medicinal: Alfalfa is rich in vitamins A, E, and D, and has an abundance of iron. This makes alfalfa supplements beneficial for joint problems and bodybuilding.

Culinary, Crafts: Many people include alfalfa in salads, as part of sandwiches, and in stir-fries. For the latter, add the sprouts just before serving so they don't overcook and mush.

Gardening, Habitat: Alfalfa grows near streams and wet meadows in Europe, North America, and West Asia.

Aloe
Aloe vera

Folk Names: Curacao aloe, Barbados aloe, water soldier

History: Aloe originated in Africa.

Folklore, Superstition, Magic: Cleopatra attributed her beauty to regular aloe treatments.

Medicinal: Apply the clear juice of the upper leaves to burns, scratches, and other minor skin irritations. The yellowish juice from the lower leaf makes an effective laxative but should never be used externally or during pregnancy. Its laxative action can cause uterine contractions.

Culinary, Crafts: Use aloe's clear juice as part of soaps and skin creams for regular skin conditioning.

Gardening, Habitat: While aloe grows wildly in the tropics, it is very hardy and can be cultivated almost anywhere. It makes a terrific house plant, especially for the kitchen, as the juice of its leaves can be applied quickly to minor burns.

Aloe prefers its soil to be sandy loam with a little peat and fertilizer. Place the soil on top of brick shards or small stones for drainage. Aloe requires little water to survive.

Other: In the language of flowers, it represents grief or bitterness.

Angelica
Angelica archangelica

Folk Names: Wild parsnip, root of the Holy Ghost, archangel, masterwort

History: Legend tells us an angel revealed to a monk in a dream that this relative of parsley could be used to cure the plague. Thus comes the name *angelica*.

Folklore, Superstition, Magic: Because of its sacred qualities, angelica was often used to cure a person of bewitchment.

Medicinal: Angelica makes a good additive to tinctures for colds or upset stomach. When the herb's roots are prepared as a tea, angelica has a warm tonic effect and improves circulation but should not be taken during pregnancy.

Culinary, Crafts: Consume angelica like a vegetable or use it to spice liqueurs and bakery items. Tea from the leaves, stem, and root tastes a bit like juniper. Try candying the stems or use the roots in bread as they do in Norway.

Gardening, Habitat: While it is native to Northern Europe, this plant adapted well to North America and Asia too. Angelica requires good moisture to grow. Harvest the leaves and stems in early summer, the seeds in late summer, and, after one year of growth, the roots in fall.

Other: Angelica is one of the herbs in Chartreuse liqueur and in vermouth. In the language of flowers, it represents inspiration, sometimes of divine origins.

Anise
Pimpinella anisum

Folk Names: Sweet cumin

History: Anise has been used since the sixth century BCE, originating in Egypt and Greece. Pythagoras believed that holding anise in one's hand alleviated seizures. Hippocrates recommended it for coughs, and the Roman scholar Pliny promoted anise as a breath freshener. This herb was so popular in the Roman empire that taxes were levied on it!

Folklore, Superstition, Magic: In Ancient Rome, anise was regarded as an aphrodisiac and hangover cure, and Virgil promoted anise as a ward against the evil eye. People in the Middle Ages often accredited this herb with the ability to preserve one's youthfulness and keep nightmares away. For the latter, place an anise flower under your pillow.

Medicinal: Quaff anise tea for sleeplessness, coughs, and as a digestive aid. Use one teaspoon of herb steeped in one cup of boiling water for about ten minutes. During hot summer months, chill and serve over ice with a sprig of mint.

For colds, take three teaspoons of crushed anise tied into a piece of cheesecloth, three teaspoons of sugar, and a half cup of water. Bring this to a boil and continue cooking over a

Patricia Telesco ────────o

low flame until syrup forms. Remove the cloth and discard the herb. Mix the syrup with one or two tablespoons of honey, then store it in an airtight container. Take a teaspoonful as needed to comfort your throat.

Those who are nursing can safely add anise tablets to their diet to help increase milk flow.

Culinary, Crafts: Anise adds a unique licorice-like flavor to eggs, spinach, carrots, and coffee. Hispanic cuisine regularly uses anise in stews and soups, and it is popular for accenting sweets in Saudi Arabia and Greece.

In the United States, anise is added to a variety of liqueurs. To make your own, take three tablespoons of anise seed and crush them thoroughly. Put them into a half-gallon glass jug and set aside. Next, warm one cup of honey or sugar with one cup of water. Pour this over the anise when the sugar or honey is fully dissolved. Add a fifth of vodka, then cork and shake the jug. Age for at least four weeks, shaking daily. Strain and enjoy. This blend also aids digestion when one takes a small sip or two after meals.

Gardening, Habitat: Anise fares well in dry, sunny soil, ideally by a hill offering good drainage. Sow the seeds in April for the best results.

Other: Add crushed anise seeds to sachets and potpourri. Give a little to your dog—they love it, and it helps offset dog breath!

Apple
Malus spp.

Folk Names: Silver bough, fruit of the gods
History: In ancient Rome, people used raw apples mingled with cloves and oil as a beauty treatment. According to legend, the apple inspired Newton's law of gravity.

Folklore, Superstition, Magic: Apples play an important role in the legends of many peoples, including the Arabs, Teutons, Celts, and Greeks. In some instances, it is a divination device, a love charm, and a symbol of fruitfulness.

Apples are also a symbol of life and death, having caused humankind's downfall in the Garden of Eden and, in the Nordic Tradition, serving as the fruit of immortality. When King Arthur dies in Celtic legends, he is taken to Avalon—whose name means "Isle of Apples" —and in *The Arabian Nights,* Prince Ahmed's apple cures any illness. In China, the apple is regarded as a fruit of peace and unity.

If you have an apple-shaped birthmark, a Western European folk tradition says rubbing it with an apple will make it disappear.

Medicinal: An apple a day keeps the doctor away! Eating a washed, unpeeled apple daily before bed aids your overall health, especially sleep. For children, very ripe grated apples offset diarrhea.

To prepare homemade apple juice, slice three unpeeled apples into one quart of spring water and boil for fifteen minutes. Strain and keep refrigerated. Warm with honey for hoarseness or a cough, or drink as is to offset gas and improve energy.

Apply an apple poultice to sore bruises. Apple vinegar combed through the hair eases an itchy scalp.

Culinary, Crafts: In addition to its traditional uses in baking and as a fresh fruit, try adding finely chopped apple to a salad with dandelion leaves and mint. I also recommend apple juice as part of pork or chicken marinades and sauces.

To make baked apples, begin with slightly sour apples and carefully remove and discard the stem, seeds, and skin to leave a cup-shaped shell. Place the apples in a greased cooking pan, then fill each center with brown sugar, topping off with a tablespoon of butter. Bake them in the oven at 300 degrees Fahrenheit until cooked through. Serve with a heavy cream drizzle.

Gardening, Habitat: A native of Europe and Asia, apples have approximately three thousand varieties. Regular pruning improves fruit production, as does sod mulch around the base of the tree.

Other: In the language of flowers, the apple represents temptation, while its flower symbolizes preference.

―――――――

Ash
Fraxinus excelsior

Folk Names: American basket wood

History: This shade-giving tree is a member of the olive family (alongside the lilac, jasmine, and forsythias). Its Latin genus name, *Fraxinus,* means "separate," alluding to the easy way the wood splits when chopped. According to the Icelandic *Prose Edda,* there was a mighty ash tree crowned with an eagle where the gods hold court.

Folklore, Superstition, Magic: Among the Teutonic tribes, the fabled World Tree, Yggdrasil, was an ash. The Norse believe that Odin, the chief god, made the first man from an ash tree. Ares, the Greek god of war, gave warriors ashen poles as weapons, and the Amazons made their spears from this wood, as did Achilles. In the British Isles, a witch's broom was believed to be made of ash wood to protect her from drowning, similar to the carved piece of ash carried by a sailor.

The leaves of this tree are considered protective and can inspire prophetic dreams. For the latter purpose, place a few beneath your pillow. Carry them with you to encourage love or pick one for luck.

Ancient Irish sailors carried ash as an amulet to protect them from drowning, and in Europe, people believed that a sickly child would be healed if passed through a cleft in an ash tree. In the Scottish Highlands, nurses placed an ash log on the fire when a baby was born. They then gathered the sap for the baby to provide protection and a long life.

Medicinal: In folk remedies, ash leaves help alleviate maladies when a water basin is placed next to a sickbed and discarded daily. During the Middle Ages, ash leaves steeped in beer were used to cure stomach disorders. The next time you get a bug bite, try applying a leaf dampened with warm water.

Culinary, Crafts: Soak small twigs in warm water, then fashion circlet wreaths to safeguard the health and well-being of one's home. Additionally, ash wood is not commonly affected by household pests, making it serviceable for tool handles and furniture making. Beyond this, thin strips of ash wood make excellent woven baskets.

Gardening, Habitat: There are over thirty species of this tree, predominantly in North America and Northern Europe. It prefers limestone-rich, damp soil.

Other: If you live in an area with many snakes, spread ash wood on the ground around your home. They will not crawl over it. The burnt ashes from ash trees were once used to make lye. In the language of flowers, this tree represents grandeur.

Asparagus
Asparagus officinalis

Folk Names: Sparrow grass
History: Egyptians cultivated asparagus over four thousand years ago as a diuretic, making a decoction from the root.
Folklore, Superstition, Magic: Carrying asparagus root protects the bearer from aching teeth. Eating asparagus improves virility, especially in men.
Medicinal: Chew the root for pain relief.
Culinary, Crafts: Asparagus blends well with lemon juice, cheese toppings, onion butters, shrimp stir fry, and ham. I'm

somewhat of a purist with my asparagus, liking it unadorned with just butter and salt. For a little more taste, try the following recipe as a side dish:

- o   2 lb asparagus, fresh
- o   1 cup white sauce
- o   1 tsp grated orange rind
- o   ¼ cup slivered almonds
- o   1 orange, juiced
- o   Salt to taste

Begin steaming the asparagus until tender. Meanwhile, prepare your white sauce, adding the orange juice, rind, and almonds after it has thickened. Pour over the asparagus before serving.

Gardening, Habitat: Asparagus thrives in temperate regions, doing best when planted between short-season vegetables like radishes in well-fertilized, loamy clay soil. Sow in fall and harvest in spring, taking the roots after the main plant.

———————

Avocado
Persea americana

Folk Names: Alligator pear
History: Central Americans and Mexicans made use of this fruit for thousands of years, mostly for food.
Folklore, Superstition, Magic: In ancient Mesoamerica, avocado was considered an aphrodisiac. The pit carried as an amulet drew love and beauty.
Medicinal: Use avocado decoction for diarrhea. Apply avocado oil or an avocado facial mask to soothe the skin. Avocado leaves and bark have historically been used to induce abortions but be careful using them during pregnancy because they might cause a miscarriage.

Culinary, Crafts: Avocados are rich in nutrients and low in cholesterol. Guacamole is perhaps the most popular use of avocados. To prepare, peel and mash one good-sized avocado. Add a half cup of diced peeled tomato, an eighth cup of chopped onion, an eighth cup of cooked chopped bacon, a dash of garlic, lemon juice (if desired), and two to three tablespoons of salad dressing or olive oil to make the mixture scoopable. Serve chilled, garnished with chili peppers and grated cucumbers.

Gardening, Habitat: The avocado is native to Central America and thrives in regions that do not experience frost conditions to grow. It prefers rich, well-drained soil and should be planted thirty inches apart. Harvest the leaves as needed and the fruit when fully grown.

Other: In Guatemala, people use avocado to increase hair growth.

Balm
Melissa officinalis

Folk Names: Bee balm, lemon balm, sweet balm, honey plant, cure-all

History: Both Pliny and Dioscorides illustrated this herb and recommended it for bringing joy and treating infected wounds. Paracelsus called it the *elixir of life,* believing balm was a tonic for memory, depression, and nervousness.

Balm's scientific name comes from the Greek word *melissa,* which means "bee," because balm flowers attract a plethora of these insects.

Folklore, Superstition, Magic: According to tradition, balm restores youth, uplifts weary spirits, prolongs life, and miraculously heals wounds.

Medicinal: Balm tea reduces fever and calms the nerves. To make a remedial balm cordial, steep a half ounce of macerated balm, mint, basil, lemon zest, clove, and sage in a liter of ninety proof consumable alcohol (e.g. scotch, bourbon, vodka) for two weeks, shaking daily. Strain and take as a remedy for indigestion or to offset menstrual cramps.

Culinary, Crafts: Balm has a mild lemon flavor that enhances poultry, jellies, and some beverages. Try mingling diced orange slices, honey, French dressing, and chopped fresh balm leaves as a baste or serving sauce for duck.

Gardening, Habitat: Native to the Mediterranean, balm prefers wet, hot conditions but can be grown well in a garden. When the plant first blossoms in early summer, the aerial parts should be harvested and dried in the shade.

Other: In the language of flowers, balm represents social conversation.

Banana

Musa sapientum

Folk Names: None.

History: Indian chronicles mention bananas as early as 2000 BCE. The fruit was introduced into Polynesia around 1000 CE and did not become widely available in Western Europe until the late 1800s.

Folklore, Superstition, Magic: In Tahiti, people sometimes offered bananas to the gods. According to Polynesian mythology, bananas sprang from human remains after the sky separated from the earth. The Bantu sometimes bury human afterbirth under banana trees to link the child's spirit to the tree.

Altars in marriage rituals in India often include bananas to ensure continued blessings for the couple.

Medicinal: Cubans dry banana leaves and make them into syrup to treat coughs. Eating unripe bananas reduces diarrhea.

Culinary, Crafts: Bananas have more culinary applications than one might expect. Try them mingled with sweet potatoes, as part of a glaze for ham or chicken, as an additive to milkshakes, or baked into bread. Bananas are also used in brewing, but decocting the flavor may sometimes frustrate the home hobbyist.

For an interesting dessert, slice bananas in half and roll them in a light mixture of flour, cinnamon, and ginger. Fry these briefly in shortening, then serve with a garnish of banana-flavored whipped cream and a slice of pineapple.

Gardening, Habitat: Native to tropical and subtropical regions, bananas require rich, well-drained soil with partial shade and wind protection. The fruit is harvested before ripening for export to other parts of the world.

Other: The banana is associated with fertility and procreative power. By extension, carrying the fruit or flowers from this tree increases abundance.

Barley
Hordeum districhon

Folk Names: None.

History: Barley has been eaten since Neolithic times and has been used in all sorts of consumables, including breads, breakfast foods, and brewing. A Babylonian beer recipe from 2800 BCE includes barley as an ingredient.

Folklore, Superstition, Magic: Egyptians offered barley to Ra, and Indians used barley during important rites of passage. Pliny recounts a magical cure for boils by applying nine grains of barley to the afflicted area, then burning the grains. In China, people once ate barley to ensure fertility.

Medicinal: Barley water mixed with warm milk aids digestion and makes a good convalescent beverage. Use a warm barley poultice mixed with honey and a few drops of lily oil against inflammation. Research shows this plant may reduce the risk of diabetes.

Culinary, Crafts: Barley is high in vitamin B and best known as a constituent in thick soups. It also makes for hearty stews. To prepare beef barley stew, preheat the oven to 350 degrees Fahrenheit. Meanwhile, add two cups of barley to two cups of beef broth and cook the barley until tender (about forty-five minutes). In a separate pan, lightly fry one small, chopped onion two stalks of celery, one cup of finely chopped broccoli, one clove of garlic, and one cup of diced beef.

Mix this with the barley mixture, then blend in a half cup of sour cream and three-quarters of a cup of grated Swiss cheese. Bake in oven for forty-five minutes and serve with a fresh garnish of cheese or buttered breadcrumbs.

Gardening, Habitat: A native plant to the Mediterranean, barley grows in temperate regions, and its seeds are harvested at maturity in the fall.

Other: In the Bible, barley sometimes represents jealousy. When made into bread, it symbolizes poverty.

Basil
Ocimum basilicum

Folk Names: Witch's herb, St. Joseph's wort (not to be confused with St. John's wort), garden basil, *tulasi* (India)

History: The herb is believed by some to have derived its name from the basilisk, a ferocious beast of legend with brutal breath. Basil originated in Africa, Asia, and India. It is dedicated to the goddess Lakshmi, the wife of Vishnu, the god that sustains life. In India, the dead are sometimes buried with basil to ensure their safe passage into paradise.

Galen and Dioscorides thought basil was poisonous, while Pliny recommended it. The Greeks and Romans thought cursing while planting basil was required for the plant to grow.

There are dozens of varieties of basil from which to choose. Lemon basil has pale, green leaves and a strong lemon scent. Cinnamon basil has a hotter flavor and resembles sweet basil.

Folklore, Superstition, Magic: Salome put the head of John the Baptist in a pot of basil. Perhaps this is how it came to represent hatred in the language of flowers. Conversely, folk traditions claim basil allays hatred and is an herb of devotion. In Italy and Moldavia, basil is a love herb, which ensures affection when gifted.

Some Hindus place basil on altars honoring Krishna. The medieval Europeans believed that pounded basil placed under a stone turns into a scorpion. If basil was held in a laboring woman's hand with a swallow's feather, it was believed to stop pain. During the Renaissance, people smelled basil to restore and cheer spirits.

Medicinal: Basil is a member of the mint family and can be used similarly to mints. As a tea, it eases digestion, cramps, flatulence, and flulike symptoms. It is also sometimes prescribed for sleep disorders, tension, and headaches. Camphor basil is used in treating colds.

Both Dioscorides and Galen wrote of basil's medicinal qualities, specifically in treating bug bites. Make a poultice of basil and apply it directly to skin sores. This is a mild antibacterial that soothes bee stings.

In Ayurvedic medicine (a form of medicine originating in India), physicians prescribe basil for fevers, typically mixed with ginger and honey.

Culinary, Crafts: Basil has a slight peppery flavor with notes of clove and mint. Fresh leaves can be frozen for later use and are best stored in oil, making it an exceptionally serviceable herb in the winter kitchen. Crumbled leaves are an excellent addition to salads. Mix basil with other herbs and butter over vegetables for zest. Don't forget to add a leaf or two to your barbecue!

Pesto is one of the best dishes with basil, perfect for romantic Italian dinners. To prepare, mix a half cup of fresh basil with one and a half tablespoons each of ground walnuts and Parmesan cheese. Add two to three tablespoons of freshly crushed garlic and purée the entire blend with a little olive oil for consistency and texture. Toss with pasta, dab on seafood, put a teaspoonful in your soup stock, or add to vegetables.

Gardening, Habitat: Basil is native to India and will grow in warm, temperate regions usually on riverbanks. It prefers sunny, warm positioning and rich soil. Sow seedlings after the threat of frost passes. Pinch off flowers regularly to increase the number and scent of the leaves.

Other: Plant basil around your home to help keep flies away and attract love to your home. Taking a bath with basil increases energy, while rinsing hair with basil tea adds luster.

———

Bay
Laurus nobilis

Folk Names: Daphne, sweet bay, lorbeer, laurel
History: This herb's Latin name means *renowned bay*. The ancient Greeks and Romans often adorned victory crowns with bay leaves and honored scholars with this plant. During the Greek festival celebrating peace, known as the *Daphnephoria*, bay leaves were a common decoration. In 342 BCE, bay laurel leaves were depicted on Roman coins. The terms *bachelor* and *laureate* come from the ancient French practice of crowning physicians with laurel berries.
Folklore, Superstition, Magic: In Greek mythology, the laurel tree was originally Daphne, a nymph pursued by Apollo. Her father turned her into this plant to protect her, at which point Apollo immediately declared it a sacred tree. To this day, the bay remains a symbol of love, devotion, success, and greatness.

Carrying bay leaves invokes the gift of prophecy and protects you from nature's furious storms. Similarly, when negative energy nips at your heels, stand near a bay laurel, and no harm can befall you. Carrying bay acts as a good luck charm.

If a bay tree dies on someone's property, it is a bad omen.

You can write a wish on a bay leaf, burn it, and let the smoke carry your wish into Apollo's ear.
Medicinal: Bay leaf was another popular herb in the Middle Ages, used for everything from bee stings to colds, menstrual irregularity, earaches, and bruises. It is still considered effective against flatulence.

For sore muscles and joints, make a bay oil to ease pain. Some people purchase the oil commercially at cooperatives. However, it can be made at home. Simmer a handful of leaves in just enough almond oil to cover them. Keep the heat low so that the leaves don't darken. When they are nearly transparent, wring them into the remaining oil and discard the leaves. Keep the oil in an airtight container. Test on a small area before applying liberally, as it can cause some problems for people with sensitive skin.

Culinary, Crafts: Soups, stews, sauces, and pickles regularly include bay as an ingredient. Add one or two leaves to cooking water when making pasta, rice, or any grain. Rub the skin of a roasting chicken with bay oil made with olive oil (prepared the same way as the medicinal application) for a flavorful treat that keeps the meat moist.

In some parts of Asia, bay leaves are added to coffee.

Gardening, Habitat: Bay grows as a bush throughout Mediterranean regions. In southern England, bay laurel is commonly cultivated in tubs, and cuttings are taken from shoots in July. Once harvested, the leaves can be dried slowly to improve their aroma. The strength of the flavor of each leaf depends on its position on the plant, harvest time, and drying duration, so use them sparingly and add more as needed.

Other: Bay leaf tea makes a good rinse to alleviate dandruff, and bay leaves added to bathwater aid relaxation. Large, sturdy bay leaves make excellent craft accessories. Lay bay leaves on picnic food or place two in your flour canister to repel insects. In the language of flowers, bay represents the change that comes with death, and in Britain, this herb symbolizes resurrection.

Bayberry
Myrica carolinensis or cerifera

Folk Names: Myrtle, candleberry, wax myrtle
History: In Scotland, bayberry leaves were once used like hops for flavoring beer.
Folklore, Superstition, Magic: If a bride plants this herb and it takes firm root, the marriage will be long and happy. This custom

may have originated from a Greek myth that describes a garland of myrtle preceding Aphrodite as she emerged from the waves. This association also connects the plant with love and beauty.

Medicinal: In North America, the roots were boiled to ease a headache and used the bark in a poultice to combat jaundice. Gather the root in fall, removing the bark and drying thoroughly before powdering. Add one teaspoon of the powder to boiling water to combat diarrhea.

Culinary, Crafts: Boil the berries until their wax rises to the surface. Use the wax to make bayberry candles or as an additive in other aromatics, like soap and incense.

Gardening, Habitat: Bayberry is native to a stretch of North America from Canada to Florida. Companion-plant bayberry with rhododendron on a dry, sandy slope.

Other: Bayberry is an effective moth repellent. In the language of flowers, it represents fertile love.

Bean
Phaseolus vulgaris

Folk Names: Poor man's meat

History: There are over 150 species of beans in the world, some with religious and folkloric significance. For example, historians believe the Oracle at Delphi often included beans as part of divinatory rites.

Folklore, Superstition, Magic: In Roman traditions, beans are a suitable food for the dead. The Japanese celebrate a festival where beans are strewn to banish all sickness and negativity while drawing good luck to the home. Folktales are filled with magical beans, many of which sprout miraculously, carrying the hero into the heavens.

Medicinal: Today, research indicates that powdered or infused beans may reduce blood sugar levels. The pods have a mild diuretic effect; try consuming them raw or in stir-fried dishes. To ease skin irritation, apply a bean poultice to the afflicted area.

Culinary, Crafts: Beans are a good source of iron and vitamins. To prepare a side dish, begin with one pound of fresh green beans cooked for fifteen minutes in water. Combine in a bowl with ten cherry tomatoes cut in half, a quarter cup of olive oil, one diced onion, a twist of lemon, and a teaspoon of dill. Serve hot or cold garnished with feta cheese.

Gardening, Habitat: Beans may have originated in South America, but they are now grown around the world. The beans are gathered in summer for food. Beans enrich the soil but cannot be planted during long bouts of below normal temperatures because a chill stunts growth or decays the seed.

Other: Dreaming of beans portends a quarrel on the horizon.

Beech
Fagus sylvatica

Folk Names: Boke, faya

History: The genus name of *Fagus* comes from *fago,* which means "to eat," likely alluding to the beechnut. The word *book* derives from beech, which is one of the earliest woods used for bindings. In the immortal words of Thoreau, "No tree has so fair a bole or so handsome an instep as the beech" (Emerson 31).

Folklore, Superstition, Magic: In Greek mythology, Jason's Argo was carved from beech and Dionysus preferred to drink wine from beech bowls. Some of the prophetic trees at Dodona in Greece may have been beeches. Beech is also a wishing tree. Carve your desire in a fallen branch and either bury it or throw it into running water for manifestation.

Medicinal: Chew a beech leaf for sore gums or apply a slightly macerated leaf to a blister for relief.

Culinary, Crafts: Use beechnuts to flavor venison.

Gardening, Habitat: This hardy tree is a member of the oak and chestnut family. It prefers northern temperate zones, and semidry soil rich in limestone.

Other: The oil in beechnuts is helpful to squirrels, blue jays, wood mice, woodpeckers, and deer, fueling their warmth through the winter months.

Benzoin
Styrax benzoin

Folk Names: Benjamin, gum benzoin, spice bush, wild allspice, fever bush

History: The berries of the *Benzoin aestivale* were used during the Revolutionary War as an allspice substitute. People prepared benzoin leaves as tea during the Civil War, and the Asiatic species is prized for making aromatic toothpicks.

Folklore, Superstition, Magic: In some spiritual traditions, benzoin is used for purification.

Medicinal: Add benzoin to inhalations for cold and sinus complaints. It has antiseptic and expectorant qualities.

Culinary, Crafts: Benzoin is an effective fixative to many aromatics and often becomes part of the base for incense.

Gardening, Habitat: Benzoin is happiest in wet conditions, like rain forests and in soil with peat and sand. It is harvested after seven years for its bark, which produces a gum.

Other: Use freshly cut branches to spice the air.

Birch
Betula alba

Folk Names: Lady of the woods, berke, beth, white birch

History: The birch rod was used to spank the bottoms of ill-behaved children, especially during the late Middle Ages. Its name may have derived from the Sanskrit word *bhurga,* which denoted a type of bark used for writing. Russians used birch wood to make torches and used birch oil to lubricate squeaky wheels. In Europe, birch branches were used in traditional boundary festivals to beat away unwanted influences around a person's home and land.

In the Celtic tree calendar, birch begins the year.

Folklore, Superstition, Magic: In Norse mythology, the final battle between the gods takes place beneath a birch tree. In Sweden, the emergence of birch leaves signals to farmers to sow barley. Russians believe that hanging a red ribbon from a branch of this tree will protect against the evil eye, and witches' broom handles were said to be made of birch. Carrying birch bark turns away thunder and evil spirits.

Medicinal: As a tea, birch bark and leaves have analgesic effects and are a serviceable mouthwash. Birch oil or sap may be applied externally to massage sore muscles. Black birch leaves relieve headaches.

Culinary, Crafts: Sweet birch, *Betula lenta,* has a minty flavor when the branches are tiny and young, and wintergreen oil is distilled from them. In the spring, the inner bark of this tree can be carved into long, thin strands like noodles and then dried. These are edible when boiled and store well. Try seasoning eggs with powdered inner bark or use as a flavoring for homemade bread. These branches may be used to make birch beer and wine, similar to those from the *Betula alba.* Here is one recipe:

- 1 qt small, freshly picked birch twigs
- 1 gallon water
- 2½ lb sugar
- 1 slice orange
- ½ package wine yeast (or beer yeast)

Clean the twigs of any debris or insects, then break them into smaller pieces before placing them into a large pot. Cover with water and allow to simmer for thirty minutes. Next, add the sugar and stir until dissolved. Turn off the heat and put the orange slice in the pot to soak until the mixture is lukewarm. Meanwhile, suspend the yeast in a quarter cup of warm water and place this in a gallon jug. Once the birch mixture cools, strain it into the gallon jug. Let sit with a porous cloth for forty-eight hours. Put a cork in gently (or screw on a top only partially) for the next two months. Tighten the top slowly, then age another four months and enjoy.

Gardening, Habitat: Found in many climates, the birch is a hardy tree that can grow even in arctic zones.

Other: Birch leaves may be made into an infusion and rinsed through the hair for general conditioning. In the language of flowers, birch represents grace and meekness.

───────

Blue Cohosh
Caulophyllum thalictroides

Folk Names: Papoose root, yellow ginseng, snake root
History: Blue cohosh grows wild in Eastern North America and was used readily by many Native American tribes to ease childbirth and as contraception.
Folklore, Superstition, Magic: Carried, worn, or kept around the house, this herb promotes love and bravery.
Medicinal: Decoctions of the root and rhizome ease menstrual cramps, while a tincture speeds a child's delivery. *Warning:* Do not use blue cohosh during pregnancy; it stimulates the uterus and may cause a miscarriage if used improperly.
Culinary, Crafts: The seeds of this plant in decoction form make a beverage like coffee.

Gardening, Habitat: Blue cohosh is a member of the barberry family and does well in areas with diffused sunlight and moist soil. Gathering this herb in the wild is easier, but if you wish to grow it yourself, take a piece of root late in fall and nurture it indoors, before transplanting it next spring.

———————

Borage
Borago officinalis

Folk Names: Miner's candle, talewort, cool tankard, burrage, bugloss

History: A time-honored symbol of courage, both Dioscorides and Pliny believed this herb was the *nepenthe* mentioned by Homer.

Crusaders introduced borage to Europe, where John Parkinson remarked that the flowers appeared in cordials and candies by the 1600s. This was a favorite flower for needlework patterns around the same time. A couple centuries earlier, Christopher Columbus sowed borage on Isabella Island.

Folklore, Superstition, Magic: During the Middle Ages, people believed that borage not only endowed bravery but also negated melancholy and brought joy.

Medicinal: Borage tea improves the flow of milk, especially when mixed with fennel.

Culinary, Crafts: Tasting and smelling like cucumber, borage adds an interesting flavor to salad dressings, especially creamy types. Boil the leaves like spinach or add the flowers to the top of a cold summer beverage for an uplifting aroma. Mingle fresh herb in a cup of wine, beer, or brandy with a twist of lemon for a zesty summer drink.

Gather young leaves and dice them finely as a stuffing for ravioli or place the flowers whole into ice cubes for a whimsical effect.

Gardening, Habitat: Borage grows well almost everywhere and is often found among weeds. It may be used as a honey plant and will grow nicely as part of rock gardens.

Other: In the language of flowers, borage represents bluntness or bravery.

Broom
Sarothamnus scoparius

Folk Names: Besom, Irish tops, link, genista, banal

History: Broom gets its species name from the word *sacopa,* the Latin word for "broom," because of its use in domestic cleaning. Some kings, including Henry II and Richard III, displayed the broom on their armor and shields as a heraldic device because it could take root in even the rockiest soils.

Folklore, Superstition, Magic: In earlier times, people drank an infusion of broom to improve prophetic abilities, but this practice is dangerous due to broom's toxicity. Broom flowers released to a light breeze will continue the wind or increase it. Hung in the home or carried, broom protects against evil influences.

Medicinal: While not recommended for the home practitioner, broom blossoms have been used to treat irregular heartbeats and to decrease blood loss after childbirth, as broom can cause uterine contractions and decreased heart rate.

Culinary, Crafts: Broom tops may be pickled with tarragon, having been served this way for the coronation of James II. In the Middle Ages, people also added the flowers to wine, or to salads with nasturtium, walnuts, raisins, and orange peel. Again, this practice is not suggested today, as large amounts of broom are toxic.

Gardening, Habitat: A native of Europe, this plant grows well in open woods and near roadsides. Gather the flowers throughout the summer and early fall.

Other: In the language of flowers, broom represents organization and modesty. The flowering tops may be gathered for yellow dye.

———————

Burdock
Arctium lappa

Folk Names: Beggar's buttons, cockleburr, hardock, clotbur, hurr-burr, turkey burrseed

History: During the seventeenth century, Culpeper recommended using burdock for gout, as did many other herbalists of the day. Shakespeare had a poor opinion of it, however, using it as an emblem of annoyance or meager fortunes.

Folklore, Superstition, Magic: Magically, burdock is considered a protective herb because of its spiny appearance. Place burdock leaves on your wrists and ankles to drain away the power of a fever or keep burdock near a baby to protect them from colic.

Medicinal: A poultice made from burdock seeds eases boils while the root can be applied to acne and psoriasis. In parts of East Asia, healers use the seeds similarly to draw out infections, and burdock root in tea mixed with dandelion acts as a cleansing agent.

Culinary, Crafts: Until about one hundred years ago, burdock was consumed as a vegetable in Japan and parts of Europe. The root was peeled, chopped, and steamed for a half hour, or the leaves and shoots were cooked similarly to spinach. In America, burdock sometimes appears as an ingredient in ale, mixed with chamomile and ginger.

Burdock may be used in brown dye.

Gardening, Habitat: Native to both Asia and Europe, burdock grows well in loose, well-drained soil and plentiful sunlight. Harvest the leaves or fruit during summer and the root in fall.
Other: For oily complexions or pimples, make a decoction of burdock and dandelion root (one cup of water, four teaspoons of dandelion root, and one teaspoon of burdock root) and drink twice a day. Alternatively, make an infusion of the seeds and wash your skin with it daily.

Cabbage
Brassica oleracea

Folk Names: Poor man's doctor, gift of heaven
History: Ancient Greeks fed cabbage to expectant mothers before delivery to increase milk flow, while the Romans used it to deter drunkenness. At the turn of the twentieth century, the heart of a cabbage was employed as a brush for household chores, like cleaning carpets.
Folklore, Superstition, Magic: In Greek mythology, cabbage first sprouted from Zeus's sweat. Cultivated in one's garden, cabbage ensures a happy marriage and healthy plants. In the late 1800s, it was common for parents to tell children that babies came from cabbage patches. Because of its green leafy nature, cabbage is sometimes considered a money herb, like lettuce.
Medicinal: A poultice of leaves applied warm to bruises, eczema, or problem joints eases discomfort. Leave this on for no longer than one hour.

Drink a decoction of cabbage leaves sweetened with honey to alleviate coughs. Cabbage juice is said to deter worms in children, and the leaves cooked in milk may be applied to blisters, decreasing the time it takes them to dry.
Culinary, Crafts: A tasty way to prepare cabbage is by boiling a chopped head with two to three diced boiling potatoes. When the potatoes are tender, drain the water. Transfer the potatoes and cabbage into a pan with a quarter cup of butter, a quarter

cup of olive oil, one minced onion, one teaspoon garlic, and one stalk of sliced celery. Fry everything together until lightly brown, then season with salt and pepper to taste. Such a dish was charmingly called "Bubble and Squeak," owing to the sounds it makes while cooking.

Gardening, Habitat: This biennial plant has numerous varieties, all of which prefer plentiful sunlight, fertilized soil, and damp conditions balanced with good drainage. When selecting cabbage for your garden, opt for seed packages indicating mid-season maturation, as these require less growing space. Set seedlings about twelve inches apart and pull the plant up by the root when harvesting.

Other: In the language of flowers, cabbage represents profit.

Calendula
Calendula officinalis

Folk Names: Pot marigold, marybud, holigold

History: Romans noticed that these flowers were always open on the first day of every month and thus named them calendula, after the word *calends*. *Calends* denoted the first day of the ancient Roman month, which was used to count days backwards to the ides.

Folklore, Superstition, Magic: The appearance of this flower lifts depression. In the tenth century, a recipe for fairy-seeing oil included calendula gathered from the east. If rubbed on the body before bed, calendula was also reputed to bring dreams to those needing to make decisions.

Medicinal: The orange and red petals of this flower are a mild antiseptic that deter infection. As a cream, ointment, or tincture, apply three times a day for skin conditions like eczema. As an infusion, calendula may be used as a douche to avoid yeast infections. For ringworm, drink an infusion of calendula three times daily. For athlete's foot, sprinkle three drops of essential oil into a half cup of baking soda and a half cup of orris root.

Mix thoroughly and insert this in your shoes. This remedy can also be applied to diaper rash. Culpeper believed that calendula fortified the heart.

Culinary, Crafts: Calendula was used by Elizabethans to flavor game birds, while the Dutch preferred the flowers in soups. They were also popular in making wine and as an alternative to saffron in its dry form.

Gardening, Habitat: Calendula originated in southern Europe and will flourish in nearly any temperate zone. It enjoys heat and grows well in average soil.

Other: To create a yellow dye, mix calendula flowers with alum. Rinse your hair with a tincture of flowers to bring out highlights. Do not consume this herb if you are pregnant.

Caraway
Carum carvi

Folk Names: Kummel

History: Caraway is one of Europe's oldest seasonings. Some seeds dating to over five thousand years ago were found in Switzerland, and Shakespeare mentions caraway in *Henry IV*. Persians once used this herb as currency.

Folklore, Superstition, Magic: Anything bearing a caraway seed is impervious to theft. Two lovers who exchange this herb will remain true to each other, and, for a little spice, carraway was also used as an aphrodisiac.

Medicinal: Caraway tea makes a good digestif and breath freshener after dinner. As with clove oil, caraway oil may relieve a sore tooth without clove's harsh flavor. Caraway infusions taken three times daily may increase breast milk in nursing parents.

Culinary, Crafts: Sprinkling dried leaves on salads adds zest. Prepare the roots similarly to carrots or parsnips. The seeds are best known as additives to bread, pork, beef, and stews. Caraway tastes a bit like dill and anise combined.

Gardening, Habitat: Caraway likes sunny locations at altitudes below six thousand feet above sea level. Sow the seeds in spring, knowing that you will not be able to harvest new seeds until the second summer. The young leaves, however, can be harvested in the first year.

Other: Washing dogs in a bath of caraway helps prevent mange. The aroma is said to help steady the nerves and allay dizziness.

Cardamom
Elettaria cardamomum

Folk Names: *Elaci* (Hindi)

History: Cardamom was a favorite herb in ancient Egypt for perfumery, and it appeared in Greece as early as the fourth century BCE for culinary purposes.

Folklore, Superstition, Magic: Carry or consume cardamom to draw love and passion into your life.

Medicinal: Cardamom is a perfect culinary herb, highly effective in treating digestive troubles. In Ayurvedic medicine, healers use cardamom to treat numerous conditions, including colds. In East Asia, infusions of cardamom are considered a good tonic.

Culinary, Crafts: Purchase cardamom in seed form, crushing it just before using to release the effective oils. In Saudi Arabia, Turkey, and France, people add a few seeds to coffee. Other culinary applications include flavoring pastries, goulash, veal, coleslaw, tomato soup, and cheese dips. It can also be used as a substitute for ginger. Try adding a few to candied yams.

In crafts, some people like to add the seeds to potpourri, especially the simmering type.

Gardening, Habitat: Native to India, the seeds are planted in fall, while root cuttings go into the ground in late spring. Cardamom prefers shade and moist soil. Seeds are harvested in early fall.
Other: Rinse your mouth with a tincture of cardamom after meals to freshen your breath.

Carnation
Dianthus caryophyllus

Folk Names: Gillyflower, scaffold flower, clove pink, the divine flower (American Carnation Society)
History: According to Pliny, the clove carnation was discovered in Spain during the time of Caesar. The Spanish supposedly used it for culinary purposes, liking its piquant flavor. Henry IV of France favored the pink variety. Carnation gets its name from *coronation* because it was a prevalent festival flower alongside roses.
Folklore, Superstition, Magic: In Elizabethan England, people carried carnations as a safeguard against meeting an untimely death on the scaffold.
Medicinal: During the mid-1600s, pickled carnations with vinegar and sugar were considered an appetite stimulant.
Culinary, Crafts: Carnations are edible and were favored in medieval Europe for flavoring mead, hippocras, and metheglin, the latter of which was used medicinally. They were also traditionally candied, jellied, pickled, or made into sweet water. For a unique tasting experience, chop up scented carnations and blend them with butter. Spread this on decorative crackers with a fresh petal as an accent.
Gardening, Habitat: A carnation is a florist's flower, cultivated from older shoots in sandy loam during spring and transplanted into the field.
Other: In the language of flowers, carnations represent pride and beauty.

Carob
Ceratonia siliqua

Folk Names: St. John's bread
History: Some historians believe that the locusts St. John ate were actually the seed pods of the carob plant, as they are filled with a honey-like substance. Carob husks were fed to the prodigal son. Evidence suggests that the pods also form the basis for the carat weight.
Folklore, Superstition, Magic: Carrying carob beans is believed to bring luck as a charm.
Medicinal: Egyptians used carob porridge for treating diarrhea. Dioscorides recommended it for digestive trouble.
Culinary, Crafts: Carob can be a chocolate substitute and is especially good in liqueurs.
Gardening, Habitat: Like oranges, carob prefers rich, porous soil, and warm regions. They will tolerate a mild frost. The fruit is harvested in late summer.
Other: Horses enjoy carob seeds.

Carrot
Daucus carota

Folk Names: Bird's nest, philtron, bee's nest, Queen Anne's lace
History: The carrot's origins are a mystery, but we do know they were cultivated in both Greece and Rome. Dioscorides specifically recommended carrots to regulate menstruation. In the sixteenth century, some people wore carrot leaves decoratively in their hair, and during the Victorian era, grandmothers often promoted carrots to bring a bright, rosy glow to the cheeks.
Folklore, Superstition, Magic: According to some folk traditions, carrot seeds improve virility, likely because a carrot is phallic shaped.

Medicinal: Organically grown carrots offer much to the body and for building red corpuscles. Drinking the juice of three to four carrots daily is believed to build immunity against respiratory disorders. Carrot soup is an age-old remedy for children's diarrhea. This is best made with water and a little salt, then blended for a creamy consistency.

Culinary, Crafts: Carrots are high in vitamin A and provide diversified culinary applications, including juicing, soups, hors d'oeuvres, and as a vegetable.

During the Jewish New Year, a carrot-honey side dish is served as a symbol of prosperity. To make this, begin with four cups of cooked carrots, two to three sliced apples, a half cup of honey, a quarter cup of olive oil, one teaspoon of ginger, one teaspoon of orange rind, and salt and pepper. Layer the carrots and apples in an ovenproof dish, covering each layer with a mixture of honey, oil, and spices. Cover with aluminum foil, baking at 350 degrees Fahrenheit until browned. If desired, replace two cups of carrots with sweet potatoes.

Gardening, Habitat: Carrots fare well in deep, light soil, sown twelve to fifteen inches apart. Harvest the roots in late summer, and the seeds in early fall.

Other: Do not consume carrot seeds during pregnancy. They contain an oil that stimulates menstruation.

⎯⎯⎯⎯

Catnip
Nepeta cataria

Folk Names: Field balm, catmint

History: Beloved by felines, catnip was used by the Romans as a tea, and people in the Middle Ages used it to flavor salads and meats. In colonial America, catnip was a commercial crop.

Folklore, Superstition, Magic: Two friends clasping fresh catnip between their hands will remain close forever. Placed around the home, this herb promotes improved fortunes and serendipity.

Medicinal: Catnip is an excellent addition to a tea for allaying fever or stomach cramps. As a word of caution, catnip may increase menstrual flow and therefore should not be used during pregnancy.

Culinary, Crafts: Catnip is popular in teas, and the French eat catnip shoots in salads. Try them this way with other unusual salad greens like dandelion or candy the leaves for a refreshing after-dinner mint. The flowers may also be prepared in conserves.

Gardening, Habitat: A temperate herb, catnip is hardy like all mints but likes well-irrigated soil.

Other: An old proverb says that "if you set it, cats will eat it; if you sow it, they won't know it!"

Cayenne
Capsicum frutescens

Folk Names: Red bird pepper, cockspur pepper, goat's pepper

History: Cayenne was introduced to Western civilization around the 1500s as a popular culinary herb. Although Christopher Columbus brought it with him to North America, Americans would have eventually enjoyed it since it is native to Mexico.

Folklore, Superstition, Magic: Like other hot, pungent herbs, cayenne is considered magically protective. Hang a garland of whole dried peppers in your kitchen to safeguard your home.

Medicinal: Small amounts of cayenne oil to liniment or massage creams create a warming sensation that stimulates circulation and aids in relaxation. Use carefully, as too much will burn. When mixed with willow bark in tincture form and quaffed twice daily, this combats arthritis. To soothe a sore throat or sore gums, mix a pinch with one cup of water and one tablespoon of lemon juice and gargle.

Culinary, Crafts: Cayenne lasts forever in dried form, making it a very serviceable kitchen spice. Cayenne is favored in Spanish, Mexican, Cajun, Asian, Indian, and Szechuan recipes.

Gardening, Habitat: Cayenne is a tropical plant that prefers hot, wet conditions and rich soil, but can also grow decently in other conditions. Plant them about two weeks after the last frost and give about a foot of space between each plant. Harvest the peppers in late summer and dry them.

Other: Cayenne gets its name from a Greek term that means "biting." Capsaicin, a chemical in cayenne, has many health benefits for humans, despite originally developing as a deterrent to keep animals from consuming the peppers.

────────

Celery
Apium graveolens

Folk Names: Smallage

History: Celery has been cultivated as a vegetable and as an herbal remedial for at least three thousand years in China and Egypt. It is a member of the parsley family.

Folklore, Superstition, Magic: In magic, celery seed improves prophetic ability and insight, while the stalk induces passion when consumed.

Medicinal: In China, celery-rice porridge is used to treat hypertension. Research conducted in 1992 suggests eating about four stalks of celery daily can reduce blood pressure. Celery oil, when extracted as an infusion or tincture, calms nerves and may help regulate blood pressure. For arthritis, a daily infusion of celery seed or one teaspoon of powdered seeds mixed with any meal should help. This is due to the celery seeds' diuretic effect. Both celery and its seeds help cleanse the body, the first through roughage and the second through its oils, which help flush the urinary system.

Culinary, Crafts: Celery is an excellent juicing vegetable, especially when blended with carrots and tomatoes, or ginger with a little honey.

Gardening, Habitat: Celery grows wild in parts of Europe, specifically England and Wales, near marshes and coasts. It cultivates well in most moist soils. Plant celery in spring and harvest in late summer or early fall.

Chamomile
Chamomilla recutita

Folk Names: Manzanilla, sweet chamomile, ground apple, plants physician, pin heads, scented mayweed, mother of the gut

History: The Egyptians dedicated chamomile to their gods and to the Sun because it effectively combats fevers. Dioscorides and Galen prescribed it for menstrual discomforts, and this herb was well known for treating jaundice and dropsy by Anglo-Saxon times. The German *Chamomilla recutita* is more popular for its pleasant flavor than the Roman variety.

Folklore, Superstition, Magic: Carry a sprig of chamomile to attract money or love.

Medicinal: Creams with chamomile effectively treat minor wounds, itchy or irritated skin, and diaper rash. For insomnia, take a cup of chamomile tea before bed or mix one teaspoon of chamomile with one teaspoon of mint in one cup of water. This tea will also help abate hay fever, relieve indigestion, and calm the nerves. Apply a compress of chamomile to inflamed eyelids or skin irritations or add some to bathwater to combat weariness.

Culinary, Crafts: Chamomile tastes similar to tart apples. While chamomile is most popularly used in teas, it also adds a unique flavor to wine, beer, and syrup. Chamomile makes a yellow or gold dye when mixed with chrome or alum.

Gardening, Habitat: Chamomile grows wild in Europe and flourishes in most sunny temperate zones—even in rocky soil. Sow in spring and harvest the flower tops in late summer. When planted with wildflowers, chamomile releases an apple scent when treaded.

Other: In aromatherapy, the scent of chamomile helps offset stress. In the language of flowers, it represents energy. To bring out gold highlights, shampoo or rinse your hair with a chamomile-based preparation.

Cherry
Prunus cerasus

Folk Names: Sweet cherry

History: Lucullus, a Roman general, brought cherry tree bark from Pontus's kingdom into Europe, where it quickly became a favored culinary fruit and aphrodisiac. In Japan and China, the cherry blossom is featured as the flower for April. During the 1700s, silk dyers often used a cherry tree as part of their trade sign.

Folklore, Superstition, Magic: In some magical texts, cherry juice was considered an acceptable substitute for blood. Additionally, the fruit or juice was an important part of spells to attract love or increase passion. Placing a strand of hair in the trunk of a cherry tree is an old folk cure for asthma. An age-old belief cautions against swallowing a cherry pit, warning that it will surely grow a tree in one's stomach. Among Swiss cherry farmers, the surest way to ensure a good crop is by giving a new mother some cherries from the orchard to eat.

In Japanese legend, the cherry flower is the reincarnation of the princess Konohama Sakura with its petals blushing like her cheeks.

Medicinal: Since cherries are rich in vitamins and other useful hormones, amino acids, and chemicals, it doesn't take much preparation to reap their health benefits. Nevertheless, there are other ways to put them to use. To tone your skin, crush the fruit and apply it as part of a facial or place the mixture on your forehead to banish a headache. Four cups of cherry decoction daily aid in combating flu, bladder infections, and joint problems. In the southern United States, cherry bark is decocted for a cold tea.

Culinary, Crafts: Fresh cherries are delightful as part of pies and pastries or cooked into jellies. Hungarians make a unique soup out of cherries, mixed with a little cinnamon, cream, cooking wine, and water. The ingredients are blended and served hot or cold.

Gardening, Habitat: While sour cherry trees cultivate successfully in different conditions, the sweet cherry doesn't take well to overly wet soil. The latter prefers deep, pebbled loam that provides adequate drainage. Both types need about twenty feet of growing space, frugal regular pruning, and effective bug deterrents.

Other: In the language of flowers, the cherry represents a good education. Dreaming of a cherry branch portends good luck.

Chicory
Cichorium intybus

Folk Names: Wild cherry, succory, endive

History: Dioscorides was the first herbalist to write about this herb, which was first cultivated in Egypt over five thousand years ago. Due to the white juice produced by this plant, it was sometimes prescribed to nursing mothers. Queen Elizabeth I enjoyed regular chicory broths, and Thomas Jefferson planted this herb at Monticello. Chicory has been used to remove the bitterness from coffee.

Folklore, Superstition, Magic: Harvest this herb with a golden blade at midnight on Midsummer's Eve, and the bearer will gain the ability to open locks and become invisible. Carry chicory to promote hospitality wherever you go.

Medicinal: Chicory is high in vitamins and minerals. An infusion of leaves and flowers acts as a digestive tonic with a mild laxative effect. Apply whole leaves to reduce swelling. Modern research suggests chicory added to coffee may help offset the stimulating effect of caffeine.

Culinary, Crafts: Roasted chicory roots are an alternative to coffee. Young roots taste like endives and can be cooked and eaten like parsnips. Mingle the fresh leaf with dandelions for a salad.

Gardening, Habitat: Plant these as part of a clock garden since they open promptly at seven in the morning and close at noon. (A clock garden has twelve sections, one for each hour of the day.) As the day progresses, plants in each section bloom to show the time. Sow the plants about a foot apart and keep the soil well-watered and lightly fertilized. Harvest the root in spring or fall and dry it for use.

Other: Charles II of France enjoyed chicory tablets as a sweet treat. In the language of flowers, chicory represents frugality.

———

Chives
Allium schoenoprasum

Folk Names: None

History: Some evidence suggests that chives originated in Russia, where they are considered a passion-inducing food. Other historians credit their beginnings to the Chinese, who likely introduced them to Europe sometime in the 1500s. Chives were brought by the colonists to America. Gerard recommended chives to help with weight loss.

Folklore, Superstition, Magic: As with onions, chives are considered protective foods due to their biting flavor.

Medicinal: Chives are a poor but serviceable substitute for onion and may be applied with less effectiveness.

Culinary, Crafts: Use chives for flavoring cream or cottage cheese, in vinegars, or on meats for zest. Chopped finely, they make a tasty addition to any green salad mixture. Note that the small purple flowers are edible in salads or mixed into omelets.

Gardening, Habitat: This hardy plant can be started from seed but grows more quickly by dividing already mature clumps. Chives benefit from regular harvesting, so trim the plant as often as needed. Companion-plant chives with carrots, roses, and tomatoes, or a combination of all.

Chrysanthemum

Chrysanthemum spp.

Folk Names: Feverfew, pyrethrum, marguerite

History: In China and Japan, the chrysanthemum has been cultivated for almost two thousand years. It is the central emblem of the Imperial Seal of Japan, bearing sixteen petals that resemble a rising sun. Its name derives from the Greek phrase for "golden flower."

Folklore, Superstition, Magic: In Chinese legends, there is a magical fountain amidst chrysanthemums. If one finds and drinks this water, one becomes immortal. To avert divine anger, keep this flower growing in your garden. This also protects your home from wandering ghosts. Some people believe that during a full moon, fairies dance beneath chrysanthemum petals. According to a Chinese superstition, drinking chrysanthemum wine encourages longevity, improves vigor, and can even regrow lost teeth.

Medicinal: Two members of the chrysanthemum family, costmary and feverfew, both have medicinal qualities. Costmary is good in tea as an aid for digestion, and feverfew is a tonic that aids migraines and soothes itchy insect stings. If your eyes are sore and puffy, apply a poultice of chrysanthemum flowers for ten minutes. This same mixture will help clear up acne. In Korea, people use boiled chrysanthemum roots as a headache cure.

Culinary, Crafts: These are edible flowers, tasting great as a salad with French dressing or as a creamed soup flavored with salt. Use a few dried petals to give flavor and aroma to your tea and in beverage making.

Gardening, Habitat: The chrysanthemum is native to China and grows very well in the West. Separate old plants in late spring (these cannot be crowded), adding fertilizer and pinching off small flowers to encourage larger ones. Water twice a week during hot weather, protect them from frost using canvas or light mulch, and harvest in late summer.

Other: Place dried chrysanthemum petals in your linen to deter bugs and ensure freshness. In the language of flowers, this blossom represents remaining cheerful during times of adversity.

Cinnamon

Cinnamomum verum

Folk Names: Sweet wood

History: Cinnamon first appeared in Chinese writings dating back to 2700 BCE. The ancient Hebrews and Arabs used it regularly as a perfume spice, which was as valuable as gold and frankincense. Egyptians used it in embalming. As one of the spices that helped spur trade, cinnamon made its way to Europe by 500 BCE. History recounts that Nero burned a year's worth of cinnamon in his grief after his wife's death.

Folklore, Superstition, Magic: In Chinese legend, a cinnamon tree grows in paradise and grants eternal life to anyone who eats of it. The Romans considered it an aphrodisiac.

Medicinal: The Japanese use cinnamon to combat high blood pressure and fever, often in an infusion. Infusions also work well to treat cold symptoms, especially chills, since they stimulate circulation. Small amounts in food can aid digestion and act as a tonic for the digestive system. Dab a small amount of essential oil on insect bites for immediate relief and disinfection. *Caution:* Some people are very sensitive to this oil. Cinnamon stimulates the uterus, so it is not recommended during pregnancy.

Culinary, Crafts: In the kitchen, cinnamon has many applications for seasoning both desserts and main dishes. Mix the powdered herb with vanilla sugar and dust sourdough toast with it for a breakfast treat.

For a hot summer day, try this Italian recipe for spiced sherbet. Begin with one cup of sugar, four cups of water, an eighth teaspoon of cinnamon oil, an eighth teaspoon of vanilla, and a three-quarters cup of nuts (your choice). Boil the sugar and water to make a syrup. Let this cool before adding the flavorings. Put this in a cake tray in the freezer, leaving it until it begins to freeze. Put this into your blender, mixing thoroughly, then return the mix to the freezer. Repeat this procedure three times, then fold in the chopped nuts before the final freezing. Serve with a whole cinnamon stick as garnish.

Gardening, Habitat: Unless you live in a semitropical region, this herb is difficult to grow at home, needing heat, moisture, and sandy loam. It grows best in the West Indies and is harvested during the rainy season.

Other: The aroma of cinnamon stimulates the appetite. Whole cinnamon sticks make a nice addition to dry floral arrangements and wreaths.

Clove
Eugenia caryophyllata

Folk Names: Chicken-tongue spice (China), *clou de girofle* (France)
History: As early as 176 CE, Southeast Asians and Indians traded clove to Alexandria, where it quickly became a highly valued culinary and medicinal spice. In the eleventh century, one could trade a pound of cloves for two cows. During the Middle Ages, people used cloves regularly in cooking and as part of pomanders, which were worn to ward off sickness.
Folklore, Superstition, Magic: In Portugal and the East Indies, some people prepare a liqueur from cloves that is thought to bring serenity to all who smell or ingest it. If you have a lot of negative energy in your home, powder some cloves and use them as incense. Mix the clove powder with a little dry sandalwood to facilitate combustion. This incense also ceases gossip. If you're looking for a soulmate, keep a whole clove folded in your wallet to draw love.
Medicinal: The most popular use of clove is applying its oil to relieve an aching tooth. Clove oil has antiseptic qualities, making it an excellent addition to water for a mouthwash. Take care, however, as undiluted clove oil can be very harsh on the skin.

Clove tea has a mild laxative effect (using one teaspoon of the herb to one cup of water). Chewing cloves can sometimes ease motion sickness and freshen the breath. Powdered cloves mixed with honey and raspberry vinegar are recommended for asthma.

To make your own clove oil, steep one cup of cloves in one cup of warm almond oil. Leave this in a dark jar, shaking daily for one month. Strain and store in an airtight container. Clove oil may be applied to sore gums, teeth, muscles, and joints.

Since almond oil is edible, you can also use this preparation in the kitchen for flavoring.

Culinary, Crafts: Cloves have hundreds of culinary applications, including as a flavoring for ham, potatoes, sweets, and sausage. People in Greece, India, and China all favor cloves when cooking. The Portuguese make it into cordials that are said to bring comfort when consumed.

Gardening, Habitat: Clove trees grow predominantly in Madagascar and the West Indies, where they are planted during the spring and summer. They require warm, wet, humid climates. The fruit is harvested during hot, arid weather.

Other: The scent of cloves keeps moths away.

Clover
Trifolium spp.

Folk Names: Trefoil, red clover, melilot

History: The ancient Greeks, Romans, Celts, and druids cultivated and revered this herb.

In 1783, the emblem for the Order of St. Patrick in Ireland became a wreath of shamrocks. Clover is also the state flower of Vermont.

Folklore, Superstition, Magic: A myriad of superstitions about the clover exist, often tied to the number of leaves they bear. Two portend love and good relationships, and three represent protection, especially if the flower is white. A four-leaf clover brings good luck and ensures the bearer of finding treasure. If a couple eat a four-leaf clover together, their happiness is forever guaranteed. Five-leaf clovers are excellent money charms, especially if the flower is red.

Medicinal: Bathe in water scented with clover flowers to abate melancholy.

Culinary, Crafts: Clover is high in protein and calcium, making it an excellent addition to almost any diet. Clover may be made into cordials, wines, butters, teas, and vinegar. It can be pickled for salads, and the flowerets can be eaten on bread for a unique sandwich. In Scotland, clover seeds and flowers are baked into bread.

Gardening, Habitat: Clover thrives in diverse environments, from a European mountainside to a field in North America, making it hard not to grow successfully. Farmers regard clover as a sign of good soil since it adds nitrogen to the land.

Other: The mythical Brer Rabbit favored clovers as food. Pliny mentions that when clover leaves tremble and stand, a storm is on the horizon.

———————

Comfrey
Symphytum officinale

Folk Names: Knitbone

History: Comfrey has been used as a healing herb for well over two thousand years, mostly as a wound treatment. It gets its name from the Latin term *comferta,* meaning "grow together," which probably explains the folk name.

Folklore, Superstition, Magic: Carried as part of an amulet, comfrey ensures safe travel without the threat of thievery.

Medicinal: Make comfrey leaves into compresses and apply to sprains or soak the leaves for an ointment to treat bruises. A comfrey root poultice draws out boils, and a tincture will combat acne.

Culinary, Crafts: During the Middle Ages, people used comfrey leaves in soups, stews, and salads. This use has since gone by the wayside, with some concerns over potential carcinogenic attributes.

Gardening, Habitat: A native to temperate European regions and a member of the borage family, comfrey likes good soil with partial shade. The leaves and flowers should be harvested in summer and the root in fall.

Other: Farmers sometimes use comfrey as fodder.

Coriander
Coriandrum sativum

Folk Names: Cilantro, Chinese parsley

History: Coriander has been known in Asia for at least 3000 years and was mentioned in the Ebers Papyrus of Egypt in 1500 BCE. In Egypt, coriander was a funerary herb, sometimes offered to the gods. The Hebrews used coriander as part of the Passover ritual, and the Romans introduced this herb to Europe as part of vinegars and remedial treatments. Pliny suggested using coriander to treat burns and to increase milk production.

Folklore, Superstition, Magic: A person that eats coriander ensures their future children are inventive. In some cultures, coriander is used as an aphrodisiac, and in Central America, it protects against evil. The Chinese considered coriander an herb of immortality.

Medicinal: Make coriander into a lotion for aching joints or as a tea to reduce flatulence, cramps, and bad breath.

Culinary, Crafts: Coriander has a strong flavor, so add it in small quantities until you're happy with the taste. It mixes exceptionally well with lentil dishes or as an accent to turnip and salmon. The seeds, leaf, and root are also edible, the latter having a subtle nutty flavor.

Try a mixture of all three as part of a fresh tomato-mushroom salad with rice pilaf.

Gardening, Habitat: Coriander is an annual herb, easily grown from seed. Gather coriander seeds in the summer and use the fresh leaves as desired. Companion-plant it with anise.

Other: Coriander is a good honey plant but cultivate it carefully as it attracts other insects.

Corn
Zea mays

Folk Names: Maize, cornsilk

History: Corn has been a staple in Central and South America for over four thousand years. The Aztecs used it to treat dysentery and to increase milk flow. The Latin name means "cause of life," indicating its intrinsic value to our forebears.

Folklore, Superstition, Magic: A corn mother goddess figure appears in almost every culture where corn was a staple food. Native Americans used popcorn for divination, and at the turn of the century, people often hung corn in the house to ensure they would not be in want. Press a corn kernel to a wart and throw it over your left shoulder to make the wart go away. Do not laugh when planting corn as this causes spaces to form between the kernels.

Medicinal: In China, people use cornsilk to decrease blood pressure. As the Mayans and Incas did, apply a cornmeal poultice to bruises, swellings, or sores. Burn an old cob and hold the area over the smoke to alleviate itching. An infusion of cornsilk is a diuretic.

Culinary, Crafts: Corn kernels are a common vegetable and yield cornmeal, while corn shucks may be used to make Victorian-style dolls for the kitchen.

Gardening, Habitat: Corn requires warm, well-drained soil, a lot of space, and good fertilization to grow well, and is best purchased fresh from local farmers. The Iroquois believe that corn, beans, and squash should always be grown together, as they are sister crops.

Other: Corn shucks were once used for making household mops.

Cowslip
Primula veris

Folk Names: Fairy cup, lady's key, plumrocks, *cusloppe* (Saxon), paigles (nineteenth century England), *primerolle* (thirteenth-century England), bassinet, bull flower, cow cranes, drunkard, water goggles, king cups, publicans and sinners, shooting star

History: In Spain and Italy, the word for "cowslip" and "spring" are nearly synonymous. During the 1500s, it was widely used as a beauty treatment.

Folklore, Superstition, Magic: Cowslip is a traditional fairy flower, and some people believe it acts like a dowsing rod to uncover hidden treasure. Sprinkle your threshold with cowslip flowers to be left alone and turn away unwanted guests.

Medicinal: Cowslip roots have expectorant and mild diuretic qualities. The flowers in tincture form combat asthma and allergies. From the 1600s through the 1800s, recipes for cowslip syrup simples appeared in many books; they were recommended for allaying headaches brought on by heat. Do not use this plant if pregnant or allergic to aspirin as large doses can cause vomiting and diarrhea.

Culinary, Crafts: While the edible flowers' popularity dwindled after the late 1700s, cowslip can still be used in conserves, wine, mead, cheese, vinegar, stuffing, pickles, pudding, and butter. To make a cowslip salad, mingle the tender leaves with lemon or lime gelatin. While this sets, mix one cup of mayonnaise, two chopped hard-boiled eggs, and one cup of cream cheese. Spread this on the gelatin and garnish with fresh flowers.

As an aromatic, cowslip smells like anise. The scent calms overexcited emotions and improves concentration.

Gardening, Habitat: Cowslip prefers open areas and chalky soils. Harvest the flowers throughout spring and summer, and the root in fall. Since this plant is somewhat rare, cultivate your own cowslip over picking it from the wild.

Other: In the language of flowers, cowslip represents grace, perhaps due to an old legend that says the flower sprang from the ground where Peter dropped the keys of heaven.

───────

Cumin

Cuminum cyminum

Folk Names: *Jeera* (Hindi), *zira* (Hindi), *kimyon* (Turkish)

History: This is a close relative to anise and caraway. The ancient Egyptians used cumin to improve digestion and to treat colds. They also placed it on altars to honor and appease the gods. Cumin is mentioned in the Old Testament.

Folklore, Superstition, Magic: Attaching a piece of cumin to any object protects it from theft. In magic, cumin may be mixed with other herbs for banishing rituals or added to love and fidelity potions. The Greeks considered it an herb of protection.

Medicinal: In foods or teas, cumin offsets gas. In India, people mix it with onion juice for fever and make tinctures for insomnia. Mixed with fennel seed, cumin improves milk production.

Culinary, Crafts: Indian and Chinese recipes favor this herb, especially in pickling and as part of curry powder. Germans prefer it as part of bread, believing the presence of the herb would keep fairies from stealing the loaf.

Gardening, Habitat: A native of Egypt and Asia, cumin is related to the carrot plant. Harvest it in late summer.

Other: Among the Greeks, this herb symbolized cruelty.

Daisy
Chrysanthemum leucanthemum

Folk Names: Herb margaret, bruisewort, moon daisy, day's eye, thousand charms, bachelor's buttons, bairnwort, banwort, catposy, less consound, may gowan, hens and chickens, little Easter flower, silver penny, sweep

History: The name daisy combines two words, *day's eye,* because the flower turns to follow the sun over the course of a day. During the 1500s, daisies were sometimes eaten to allay hunger.

Folklore, Superstition, Magic: Sleep on the roots of this flower and errant lovers will return to you. Carry or wear a daisy to attract love. According to Christian legend, daisies grew from Mary Magdalene's tears and were sacred to her and St. John.

Medicinal: As an ointment, oil, or salve, daisy petals make an effective treatment for bruises and minor wounds. Steep two cups of petals in one cup of almond oil until the petals turn translucent. This mixture is also edible and may be used for frying.

Chew fresh daisy leaves to deter canker sores, drink tea made from petals to offset tension, or steep two cups of flowers in a quart of wine, and drink a cup daily to ease bruise-related pains.

Culinary, Crafts: Daisy petals make a lighthearted addition to salads and create a lovely wine. The leaves may be eaten fresh or cooked like a vegetable with butter and salt. For decoration, make daisy chains in spring for your home or craft chaplets for May Day celebrations.

Gardening, Habitat: Soils lacking lime benefit from growing daisies. Plant daisies in low, moist areas and cover your daisy bed with straw in the winter.

Other: In the language of flowers, the daisy represents innocence and fidelity. An old proverb says when you can put your foot on seven daisies at once, summer has arrived.

Dandelion
Taraxacum officinale

Folk Names: Swine's snout, priest's crown, blowball, milk gowan, *pissenlit* (French)

History: Dandelions originated in Greece and were used for both medicinal and culinary applications. Legend tells us that the flower sprouted from the dust raised by the sun chariot, explaining why the dandelion opens its petals at dawn and closes them come nightfall. Dandelions are documented as a diuretic in the works of Arab physicians in the eleventh century. The name *dandelion* comes from the French "dent de lion," alluding to the jagged, yellow flowers that look like lion's teeth.

Folklore, Superstition, Magic: Dandelion tea is said to increase psychic powers, possibly stemming from their symbolism in the flower language as oracles. Blow on the head of a dandelion gone to seed and let it carry your wishes, messages, and questions to the one desired. A person who rubs dandelion juice on themselves will be welcome wherever they go, receiving unusual hospitality. In Italy, dandelion flowers gathered on St. John's Eve protect the bearer from Witchcraft.

Medicinal: Rub dandelion juice to soothe bug bites. Dandelion broth eases a fever and acts as a wash for minor sores. Eating dandelions in other forms increases the appetite, but take care, as they also have a diuretic and mild laxative effect, as the folk name, *pissenlit* in French or *wet-a-bed*, suggests. Float the leaves and petals in a bath or prepare a decoction of the root to cleanse the skin.

Culinary, Crafts: Dandelions are high in vitamins A, B, and C, as well as potassium. Despite their scurrilous reputation as weeds, they may be made into beer, added to omelets, and even enjoyed battered or deep-fried.

On a hot summer day, try making a salad of dandelion leaves tossed with watercress, bacon bits, and vinaigrette. Cook the leaves and butter them with a hint of garlic. Blend freshly picked dandelion into a soup with leeks, cabbage, and potato, or dry and grind the root as a coffee substitute.

Gardening, Habitat: Like any good weed, dandelions grow profusely. If you wish to cultivate them, gather some seeds and sprinkle them merrily on your lawn or garden and then let nature take its course.

Other: A brownish red homemade dye can be created from dandelion roots. For an effective beauty treatment, pick flowers just as they open and place a cup of them in two pints of water. Boil for thirty minutes then strain and apply to freckles.

Dill
Anethum graveolens

Folk Names: Dilly, garden dill

History: The Ebers Papyrus from 1500 BCE notes dill as a painkiller. Romans and Greeks grew dill in gardens and often used it to decorate returning heroes. Its name originates from a Saxon word for *lull,* which aptly reflects its usage as a tea to put fussy babies to sleep. Dill looks similar to fennel and is a member of the same herbal family.

Folklore, Superstition, Magic: In Greece, people covered their eyes at bedtime with fronds of dill to bring restful sleep. Ancient mages burned dill to turn a thunderstorm. The Anglo-Saxons believed that dill weed protects the bearer from Witchcraft. For this purpose, one must carry a sprig over their heart. The devil cannot step foot into a garden where it grows. Hang dill in doorways to protect your home or nibble a fresh sprig to increase passion.

Medicinal: Dill tea is good for insomnia. It's more effective and easier to drink when mixed with parsley and anise. Use proportions of one teaspoon anise to a half teaspoon each of dill and parsley with two cups of hot water.

Herbalists in the United States and Europe recommend dill for breast-feeding people or people suffering from flatulence.

It is also effective against colic and cramping. Smell a jar of heady dill pickles for hiccups!

Culinary, Crafts: Dill has a sharp, aromatic bite that is excellent in salads, mixed vegetables, and sour cream garnishes. It is a favorite spice for pickling, especially in India. To make a wonderful batch of pickles that is both healthy and tasty, try this recipe:

- 6 cups vinegar
- 3 quarts water
- 1 ½ cups salt
- 1 tbsp garlic powder
- 50 cucumbers (small)
- 9–10 dill blossoms
- 15 garlic cloves
- 1 tbsp minced onion
- 5 peppercorns
- 10 bay leaves

Wash five-quart jars with scalding water. Place one to two blossoms of dill in each jar, along with two bay leaves, two to three cloves of garlic, and one peppercorn. Put about eight to ten cucumbers in each jar and set aside. Meanwhile, warm to boiling the vinegar, salt, water, garlic powder, and minced onion. Pour this over the cucumbers, leaving about a half inch unfilled at the top of the jar. Wipe the rims, place the lids on, and screw everything in place loosely. Put these jars into a rack in a kettle filled with hot water. Make sure they don't touch each other, then cover and boil for twenty minutes. Remove these carefully from the pot and let them cool completely, testing the jar's seal after twelve hours. Let pickles age for at least two weeks before eating. Chill and serve.

If you prefer a milder garlic flavor, substitute elephant garlic instead, slicing it into the size of normal cloves. For a stronger dill flavor, add an extra full dill blossom to each jar.

Gardening, Habitat: A native of the Mediterranean, southern Russia, and Asia, dill grows in abundance as a garden herb. Freeze the herb on the stem for use later. The leaf tastes best when harvested in spring and early summer, and the seeds in late summer.

Other: Oil from dill is used in scented soaps. Apples, dill, coriander, mallow, and chervil bud better when grown together. Dill also helps the growth of cabbage and onions.

Echinacea
Echinacea angustifolia

Folk Names: Purple coneflower, black sampson, hedgehog, Sampson root

History: The ancient Greeks called this plant by a name meaning *hedgehog* because of its bristly head. Echinacea grows natively in Central America and was possibly the most popular medicinal herb in the Native American pharmacopeia.

Folklore, Superstition, Magic: In some Native American traditions, echinacea is offered to invoke spirits for aid in magical works.

Medicinal: Echinacea has become one of the wonder herbs of the New Age. It strengthens the immune system and fights infection when taken as a regular tincture. A decoction of echinacea three times a day fights sore throat, and capsules treat colds, allergies, and asthma.

Some Native American remedials call for echinacea to treat insect bites. The juice is applied directly on burns or consumed with water for cleansing.

Gardening, Habitat: Echinacea is a fine landscaping flower. Plant seeds in the spring, or root divisions in winter, using a good potting soil mixed with sand. Place in a sunny location and harvest the flowers when fully opened. In the fall, pull mature roots for division and use.

Elder

Sambucus canadensis

Folk Names: Pipe tree, elderberry, old gal, nature's medicine chest

History: Throughout Europe, elder was a favored wood for burial rites and was sacred to several great goddesses because of its white flowers, which symbolized fertility. The Romans used elderberries to dye their hair and paint statues of Jupiter red. In France, elder flowers were used to pack apples to enhance the flavor. During the Middle Ages, these blossoms were added to the posset at a baptismal celebration.

Folklore, Superstition, Magic: It was believed that anyone who anointed their eyes with elder juice could see and identify witches during the Middle Ages. Elder wood was never to be burned as it would cause you to see the devil. Judas was thought to have hung himself from an elder tree, and elder was never used in cradle construction lest the fairy folk have access to the child. When planted near a home, elder protects from evil intentions and attracts fairies. Carrying a walking stick of it, however, invites slander. To rid yourself of warts, rub the area with a green twig, then bury it in the ground. If a pregnant person kisses an elder tree, it will bring good fortune to their baby.

Medicinal: Elder flower cream and water alleviate eczema and dry skin conditions. In the Middle Ages, a similar preparation was used to minimize freckles. Elder flower tea treats cold symptoms, especially the chills. The first shoots of elder when boiled in water are effective against phlegm. The juice of the leaves may help treat dry sties, sunburns, and abate headaches. Make a mixture of fresh leaves with olive oil and apply it on hemorrhoids to alleviate some of the pain. Try this both warm and cold to see what best suits your condition. Use elder flower infusions against congestion, elder flower tinctures for hay fever, and elderberries as a mild laxative.

Culinary, Crafts: The fruit of common elders is favored for wine, cider, and pie-making. The flowers of this tree can also be added to wine, simply by hanging them in a semi-full bottle for seven nights and gently squeezing to release their scent into the beverage. Note that elder flowers are edible and may be used in jam, fritters, vinegar, or syrups, adding a flavor like Muscat grapes. When the leaves are mixed with alum in water, they make a green dye; the berries, a blue dye; and the bark with an iron mordant makes a black dye.

Gardening, Habitat: Elder is a hardy tree, growing well in areas that offer good root support, drainage, and plentiful moisture. The aerial parts should be harvested in spring, and the berries in fall.

Other: The Greek wind instrument *sambuka* was made from the hollowed stems of this shrubby tree, as were needles, skewers, and combs. Shoots are also hollowed out for tapping maple syrup. Elderberries made into a decoction make a good hair conditioner, and steeped flowers produce a liquid for enhancing hand creams. If tossed into wash water, elder leaves make for a stimulating bath that repels insects. For birdwatchers, a bush elder nearby will draw numerous winged friends to view. In the language of flowers, elder represents compassion.

Elm
Ulmus spp.

Folk Names: Common elm, field elm, elven

History: Dioscorides first mentions the elm in 1 CE as a demulcent. Its name originates from the Saxon word *ulm*. In some Germanic regions, people would hold worship and court proceedings among groves of elms. In ancient Rome, elm leaves were used as cattle food, and the trees supported grapevines for making wine. There are still over forty places in England named after the majestic elm trees growing nearby. Native Americans used slippery elm (*Ulmus rubra*) as a wound poultice.

Folklore, Superstition, Magic: Growing elms near your home is said to protect it from lightning. In Europe, elves find their home in the tree, so watch for the magical folk there. If the elm leaf is fully visible, European farmers considered it safe to grow crops. For positive relationships, carry elm leaves or wood.

Medicinal: Slippery elm bark steeped in water makes an excellent gargle for sore throats and may be applied as a poultice for breathing problems. Warm milk with finely powdered elm is a gentle food for the ailing. Apply bruised elm leaves to sores and use the water in the leaves for a skin cleanser.

To make slippery elm lozenges for a sore throat, mix a quarter cup of elm powder slowly with honey until a paste forms, then add a few drops of lemon juice. Place the paste on a wooden board covered with a sprinkling of the elm powder and shape it into a long, thin roll. Cut this into pieces roughly the size of standard cough drops and bake them at 250 degrees Fahrenheit for an hour. This procedure may be applied to any powdered herb to create tablets for use.

Culinary, Crafts: Slippery elm bark makes an effective and nutritious chewing gum. When boiled down, it also makes a serviceable jelly that can be added to convalescent diets.

Gardening, Habitat: Elms are hardy and adapt to variable climates, but they are often plagued by insects and disease. To treat Dutch elm disease, destroy all infected leaves as they appear. Double-sided tape around the trunk's midpoint will allay some insect infestations.

Other: Elm is a popular wood for floors and boats because of its resiliency. When elm leaves are as big as mouse ears, farmers say it's time to plant barley.

Eucalyptus
Eucalyptus globulus

Folk Names: Blue gum tree, fever tree
History: Beloved by the koala bears, eucalyptus was used by Aboriginal Australians as a remedial for fevers, and the root was tapped as a source of water when rain was scarce. It was introduced to Europe in 1856 and placed in marshy regions to help dry the soil. Eucalyptus is one of the largest trees in the world, growing up to two hundred feet tall.
Folklore, Superstition, Magic: To avert a cold, carry eucalyptus or place a branch over one's doorway.
Medicinal: The last fifty years of research suggests eucalyptus has antiseptic qualities and can treat chest congestion. Smell for a stuffy nose or take 200 milligram capsules thrice daily for a cold. Prepare an infusion to combat sore throat or bronchitis and apply diluted oil as a chest rub when experiencing labored breathing. Eucalyptus is also a good addition to muscle and joint creams and liniments. Spray an infusion of eucalyptus in sickrooms to decrease viral spread. Place a compress on hands and feet to alleviate a fever. This also reduces discomfort from chicken pox.
Culinary, Crafts: Add eucalyptus leaves to air fresheners, pet beds, and other deodorizers. The leaves or seed pods make a lovely addition to pantry wreaths.
Gardening, Habitat: Eucalyptus grows natively in Australia and Tasmania, and may be cultivated carefully in marshy regions. They require plenty of water to survive. The leaves are harvested for their essential oil.
Other: Eucalyptus deters mosquitoes and fleas. It is poisonous to cats and dogs.

Fennel
Foeniculum vulgare

Folk Names: Hinojo, wild fennel, sweet fennel

History: The Greeks grew fennel to honor Adonis, while Roman soldiers ate it in lieu of food when time was of the essence. Both Dioscorides and Hippocrates recommended fennel for nursing, which is a recommendation that still holds merit. It was popularly used in the Middle Ages as one of the nine sacred herbs that cured disease and reduced weight. Prior to the Norman conquest, Anglo-Saxon cookbooks included recipes with fennel for the table and for health (particularly to improve eyesight). At the turn of the century, fennel appeared in Sabbath day posies, and its seeds were commonly given to restless children and sleepy farmhands to chew.

Folklore, Superstition, Magic: Fennel placed in a keyhole keeps ghosts away. To avert evil intension, hang some in the doorway of your home on Midsummer's Eve.

In the Middle Ages, farmers rubbed their cattle with this herb as a safeguard from Witchcraft. During Louis XVI's reign in France, his court sorceress, Catherine La Voisin, used fennel in her love potions. Carried in one's pocket, fennel grants strength and courage.

Medicinal: Some people believe that fennel in your diet will help with weight loss and improve memory. To ease hiccoughs, make it into tea or chew a fresh sprig. During the 1600s, fennel seed was eaten with dinner to improve digestion. A steaming decoction eases the discomfort of puffy eyes, while a cool cloth soaked in this mixture, applied three times a day, deters nervousness. Fennel capsules improve the flow of breast milk. Fennel seed decreases bloating and can be used as an infusion for an irritated throat and a syrup for teething babies.

Culinary, Crafts: The seed or the finely diced leaves of fennel taste like licorice or anise. Generally, fennel is preferred by chefs to flavor fish or sweet dishes. Eat sweet fennel stems like celery, or cook fennel roots like a vegetable, served with dressing or chive butter.

Before cooking fish, place some fennel stalks on your barbecue grill.

Gardening, Habitat: A native of southern Europe, fennel grows best on embankments and in rocky soil with plenty of sunlight. Harvest the seeds in fall.

Other: Infuse two tablespoons ground seeds in a half cup of water. Strain and add this to a half cup of yogurt with oatmeal for a pasty consistency. This is an excellent scrub for the complexion or may be applied as a paste for eight to ten minutes and then rinsed. According to Pliny, snakes eat fennel just before shedding their skin. In the language of flowers, fennel represents flattery.

———

Fig
Ficus religiosa

Folk Names: Common fig

History: Along with the olive and the vine, the fig is the most frequently mentioned tree in the Bible. The Greeks believed that Demeter gifted this tree to Phytalus, and Spartan athletes ate figs to improve their performance.

Folklore, Superstition, Magic: Some theologians speculated Eden's Tree of Knowledge was a fig instead of an apple. In Buddhism, the Buddha gained enlightenment under the branches of a fig tree. In Islam, the fig tree is sometimes called the Tree of Heaven, and, in Oceanic tradition, the Tree of Life. In Roman mythology, Romulus and Remus were born under the tree.

Medicinal: Figs have a mild laxative effect, and their pulp may be applied to swellings or abscesses. For the latter purpose, roast the figs before use.

Culinary, Crafts: Fig juice is a typical child's beverage in Greece, and the fruit is common for snacking in both fresh and dried form. For a tasty dessert, mix a half cup of sugar with a half teaspoon of orange rind, a half teaspoon of vanilla extract, a half cup of brandy, and a half cup of slivered almonds over a low flame. Stir until the sugar dissolves, then add three-quarters pound of figs. Cook until the figs are heated, then serve.

Gardening, Habitat: Figs are native to Asia. The trees will not tolerate temperatures below twenty degrees Fahrenheit and prefer moist, heavy soil with some sand.

Other: In Israel, the fig represents peace and plenty.

────────

Garlic
Allium sativum

Folk Names: Stinkweed

History: Garlic has a long history dating back to the Babylonians around 3000 BCE. It is a relative of the onion family, eaten fresh to ensure strength and health. In some regions of Egypt, garlic was briefly used for currency.

Since the Roman god of war favored garlic, Roman warriors often carried bulbs for vitality. During the Middle Ages, garlic was a main dish. In Greece, Aristotle mentioned its use as a spring tonic.

Folklore, Superstition, Magic: In Sweden, necklaces of garlic are placed on livestock to protect them from trolls. The Romans and French felt it was an effective aphrodisiac, and travelers in Greece left garlic at crossroads as an offering to Hekate. Medieval people believed garlic protected them from the evil eye, witchcraft, and all baneful spellcraft. Bullfighters in Bolivia carry it into the ring, feeling that the bull will not charge if it smells the herb, and up until one hundred years ago, Europeans hung garlic in birthing rooms to strengthen and protect people during child labor. Carry a garlic braid into a new home or when traveling by ship to protect against bad weather and malevolent magic.

Medicinal: The ancients were quick to discover many uses for garlic. The Sumerians recommended it for colds, the Egyptians for insect bites and headaches, the Indians for stamina, and the Greeks for endurance. Physicians through the Middle Ages carried garlic to protect themselves from the plague. Scientists now confirm that garlic juice is an antibacterial agent.

One teaspoon of finely chopped garlic twice daily with a full glass of water may ease arthritis, improve blood pressure, and reduce blood sugar levels. Gargling garlic water alleviates laryngitis and sore throats. Rinsing one's feet with a garlic wash eliminates athlete's foot and rubbing fresh cloves on acne will help clear the skin. A small piece of garlic placed in a cavity relieves toothache.

Garlic poultices are recommended for joint problems, bug bites, and boils. Be sure to test these poultices in a small area first to ensure your skin isn't sensitive to garlic's caustic nature. A garlic tincture has shown potential for treating hypertension, while garlic extract applied to pimples frequently clears the complexion.

To make an effective cough syrup, warm one cup of honey with four cloves of peeled garlic, a dash of rosemary, one slice of lemon, and one slice of orange. Pour into an airtight container and take a teaspoonful when needed. The syrup also tastes great as a poultry glaze!

Culinary: In my home, there is no such thing as too much garlic. In fact, it is a sacred commodity added to our soup, stews, stir-fries, butters, sauces, stuffing, vinegars, and salad dressings. If you have a jar of olive oil used for preparing meats, add a few cloves of peeled garlic for a flavorful change. This also helps preserve the garlic.

For a terrific cleansing soup, sauté eight crushed garlic cloves in two teaspoons of olive oil. As it cooks, add two slices of cubed bread to brown. Remove from heat and add to blender with a half cup of broth (your choice), two-thirds cup of white wine, and salt and pepper to taste. Blend thoroughly. Return to the pan to warm before garnishing with shredded cheese and chopped chives. Serves three to four people.

Gardening, Habitat: Plant garlic cloves six inches under the surface of your soil in September for harvesting the following summer.

Other: Mix garlic juice with castor oil and work it into your hair to improve gloss and body. Rubbing bald spots with a fresh clove of garlic supposedly stimulates hair growth. Spray roses with garlic water to keep bugs away.

⎯⎯⎯⎯⎯

Gentian
Gentiana lutea

Folk Names: None.

History: A favorite garden plant since the sixteenth century, this herb is named after a king of Illyria from the second century, Gentius, who purportedly discovered the root's medicinal value.

Folklore, Superstition, Magic: Legend has it that the Hungarian King Ladislaus I prayed for a cure to the plague and shot an arrow that lodged in a gentian plant.

Medicinal: The root from yellow gentian may be used as a tincture to improve appetite or as a decoction for anemia. In Switzerland, it is mixed with wine to improve energy and decrease the aches and pains caused by colds. This herb may cause miscarriage and should not be used during pregnancy.

Culinary, Crafts: These flowers are sometimes used as bitter flavoring in an aperitif, and the flowers are popular ornamental blossoms in European rock gardens.

Gardening, Habitat: A native to mountainous regions of Europe, gentian likes loam-rich soil that is low in lime and sheltered among other plants for shade. The roots are harvested in the fall.

Other: The aroma of gentian is said to allay panic attacks.

Geranium
Pelargonium spp.

Folk Names: Rose geranium, crane bill

History: According to Islamic legend, this flower was born from the sweat of Muhammad. While initially thought to originate from India, the plant is native to South Africa.

Folklore, Superstition, Magic: If grown in your garden, geraniums protect the home from snakes. Red flowers were grown by witches to announce the arrival of uninvited guests. Pink geraniums are used in love magic, while white ones are used for fertility. The rose geranium protects your home and brings love if rubbed on your doorway.

Medicinal: As a tonic, geranium helps calm erratic emotional states and has mild sedative qualities. The oils of this flower treat chilblains. When dabbed on the skin, the oils also keep away insects.

Culinary, Crafts: The geranium flower is edible and can be added to punches or used to flavor ice cream, apple pie, jellies, and puddings. To make a nice spread, mix eight ounces of cream cheese with four tablespoons of sugar and four drops of geranium oil, then beat them together. Use this spread on fruits or breads and freeze leftovers.

Alternatively, add fresh rose geranium petals to sugar and shake vigorously. Leave for twenty-four hours for a lovely scent. Or wrap your butter with a large petal to infuse a pleasant aroma.

Gardening, Habitat: A temperate plant that likes good soil, it may be cultivated from seed or by plant division.

Other: The scent of geranium helps people suffering from PMS. In the language of flowers, the geranium represents comfort and consolation.

Ginger
Zingiber officinale

Folk Names: African ginger, Jamaica ginger

History: Ginger likely originated in India and southern China. Over 4,000 years ago, the Greeks prepared sweet breads with ginger. Pythagoras recommended ginger as an antidote for poison. In the Middle Ages, medicinal beers regularly included ginger, often to thwart the plague. By the 1500s, the Spanish cultivated ginger for trade with the Puritans. During the 1700s and 1800s, it was one of the most popular culinary herbs throughout Europe. Ginger beers were a favorite beverage on the American frontier, having arrived in the continent via Spanish trading routes from Jamaica.

Folklore, Superstition, Magic: Plant ginger root in your garden or sprinkle powdered ginger in your wallet to attract prosperity. Ginger and roses are a popular combination in Asian cuisine to inspire love. Among the Philippines, this is a protective herb. In fishing folklore, chew ginger root and then spit on the bait to catch catfish.

Medicinal: Ginger tea is good for stomach cramps, diarrhea, and general digestive disorders. Use one teaspoon of herb to one cup of water. In this form or candied, it also alleviates motion sickness. At the first sign of a cold, drink one cup of warm milk mixed with a teaspoon of ginger and honey.

Culinary, Crafts: Ginger has a biting taste with mild citrus overtones, and there is very little in the pantry that bruised, boiled, candied, fresh, or powdered ginger can't accent. Here is one of my favorite recipes for ginger and carrot soup:

- 2 cups shredded carrots
- 2 cups water
- 2 chicken bouillon cubes
- 4 tbsp butter or margarine
- 12 inches of peeled, grated ginger
- 2 cups cream or milk
- 2 tbsp flour
- 2 tbsp sugar or honey
- 1 tbsp ginger
- ½ cup chopped chives (optional)
- 1 tbsp garlic (optional)

In a saucepan, simmer the carrots, chives, water, and bouillon together until the carrots are tender. In a separate pan, lightly sauté the ginger root and garlic in butter. Mix the cream, flour, and sugar until smooth and slowly add this to the garlic-ginger butter. Pour this entire mixture into the carrots and cook over a low flame for fifteen minutes. Add more powdered ginger to taste. Continue to stir for a smooth consistency. This recipe is also tasty served over pork chops. Yields two one-cup servings.

Gardening, Habitat: Cultivated in Africa, Asia, and India, ginger requires rich, moist soil, a warm, humid atmosphere, and shade for best cultivation. Ginger can grow indoors with good potting soil and a moist environment. The soil should include loam, sand, moss, and compost mixed well. Harvest after eight to twelve months. At that time, pull the root, cut away as much as possible, and replant the remainder.

Other: Ginger has a fresh, clean scent, making it an excellent breath freshener when candied. As a fine powder, add it to other ingredients to make an effective odor deterrent. Here is one recipe:

- ○ 1 cup corn starch
- ○ 2 tbsp orris root powder
- ○ 1 cup baking soda
- ○ 3 tbsp finely powdered ginger

Blend all the ingredients together in a bowl, then sift thoroughly twice. This yields a soft powder that can be used on the body or in shoes. Sprinkle the powder over rugs or carpets, then vacuum to freshen. Store in an airtight container. Alternatively, substitute one tablespoon of cinnamon and one tablespoon of orange or lemon powder in place of two tablespoons of ginger. This smells a lot like cookies!

───────

Ginseng
Panax quinquefolium

Folk Names: Wonder of the world root, five fingers, man's health, red berry, sang, man-root

History: Shen-Nung wrote about ginseng five thousand years ago when it was already regarded as a wonder herb that cured many ills. It was introduced to Europe via Saudi Arabia around the ninth century CE. The Native Americans and the Canadian missionaries both used this herb as a remedial. In the eighteenth century, this root was worth its weight in gold.

Folklore, Superstition, Magic: In Asia, ginseng is an aphrodisiac and promotes longevity, containing the vital essence from the Earth. The most potent roots naturally looked like a human body. Some psychics place a piece of root under their tongue to obtain the gift of prophecy and insight.

Medicinal: In Russia, ginseng is a popular antiseptic. Ginseng tea increases circulation and improves digestion. In 500 milligram capsules, ginseng reputedly increases energy, and in syrup form, it acts as an overall tonic, especially for those suffering from stress-related conditions. *Warning:* Avoid caffeine when using this herb.

Gardening, Habitat: Ginseng takes five to seven years to mature, preferring cool, fertile, moist soil with shade and drainage. Harvest the root in fall, steaming it before drying.

Other: Do not use this herb during pregnancy.

Goldenrod
Solidago canadensis

Folk Names: Sweet goldenrod, blue mountain tea, wound weed, Aaron's rod

History: The German settlers of Pennsylvania first made goldenrod tea and would export it to China.

Folklore, Superstition, Magic: In parts of the United States, people once believed that wherever goldenrod grew, buried treasure could be found. The sudden appearance of goldenrod portends good fortune. Some dowsers use goldenrod stalks.

Medicinal: Goldenrod tea reduces fever and allays nausea.

Culinary, Crafts: Goldenrod is a popular border plant in Europe. The flowers dry well for arrangements, and the tops make various types of yellow dye. It has a pleasant anise flavor and works well when combined with ginseng.

Patricia Telesco ————•

Gardening, Habitat: This native of North America prefers sunny regions with sandy soil. It grows easily in one's garden, which may cause hay fever in your housemates!

Other: In the 1940s, some creative companies marketed goldenrod as gum and candy.

———

Hawthorn

Crataegus oxyacantha

Folk Names: Mayblossom, whitethorn, quick, haw, May bush, bird eagles, valerian of the heart

History: The Greeks called it *krataigos,* which derives from the word "strength," because of its sturdiness. In Germany, hawthorn bushes marked land boundaries, and in many regions, were used as firewood because of its high heat. In the Middle Ages, the hawthorn symbolized hope due to its medicinal qualities but strangely foretold death when a branch was brought into one's home. Culpeper recommended the berries as a treatment for heart failure in the 1600s. Today, there are over a hundred types of hawthorn trees in the United States alone.

Folklore, Superstition, Magic: At weddings in ancient Athens, guests carried sprigs of hawthorn to ensure a joyful marriage. Roman men waved a branch of this above their bride's head in the bedchamber for fertility, protection, and devotion. They also tied it to a newborn's crib to keep away illness.

In the Celtic tree alphabet, hawthorn is the tree of May, representing the purity of new life. In some Christian legends, Christ's crown of thorns was made of hawthorn, as was the Glastonbury thorn planted by Joseph of Arimathea. The May Day maypole, around which wishes were woven, was made of hawthorn.

Carried in a pouch or wallet, hawthorn attracts good luck and fairy visitations. In folklore, people believed that witches

× 114 ×

could turn themselves into these trees. Carry hawthorn with you to encourage joy and successful fishing expeditions, literally and figuratively. In Turkey, if one wishes to receive a kiss, they should present a hawthorn branch to the intended individual. In Rome, the hawthorn was an emblem of marriage, and in the region of Burgundy, the scent of hawthorns is said to carry the prayers of the faithful directly to God.

Medicinal: In the Middle Ages, Europeans used hawthorn as a tonic for kidney and bladder problems. An Irish physician in the late 1800s observed hawthorn helps regulate blood flow. To this day, hawthorn infusions are still used for their cardiovascular benefits. Hawthorn berries and flowers make a soothing throat gargle in tincture form. The seeds and berries boiled into tea are good for cramps. Hawthorn water applied to the skin helps draw out splinters.

Culinary, Crafts: Of all the varieties of hawthorn, the downy (*Crataegus mollis*), native to Ohio, South Dakota, and Kansas, the black haw (*C. douglasii*), and the scarlet haw (*C. arnoldiana*) bear the tastiest fruit. The blossoms alone are especially pleasing in syrups, jams, cordials, and teas (try a slice of lemon on the side).

To make hawthorn honey, which bears a slightly almond-like aroma, steep equal amounts of petals within the honey at a low temperature until translucent. Strain and enjoy. For hawthorn syrup, replace the honey with maple syrup.

Gardening, Habitat: Hawthorn grows best in northern temperate climates and may be added to the garden or hedge as a bush. Gather flower tops toward the end of spring and the berries at the beginning of fall.

Other: Tool handles are commonly made from this wood, making it a good choice for a decorative walking stick as well. Some species of hawthorn bear edible fruit that resemble a small apple. In ancient Greece and Rome, hawthorn symbolized fertility and marriage, while in the language of flowers, it represents hope.

Hazel
Corylus spp.

Folk Names: Coll, cobnut, filbert
History: In Irish legend, the first hazel tree grew upon the Well of Wisdom and held all the knowledge of the universe within its branches. A salmon consumed nine hazelnuts from this tree and obtained omniscience. During the Middle Ages, heralds carried a hazel branch to mark their office.
Folklore, Superstition, Magic: In the Celtic tree alphabet, hazel comes ninth and symbolizes sagacity. In America, hazel rods cut on Midsummer's Eve were highly favored for dowsing, finding treasure, finding water, and divining the identity of a thief. Before making a wish, weave a crown of hazel branches to wear on your head, and your wish will come true. Place hazel branches on a horse's tether to protect it from bewitchment. Carry a double hazelnut in your pocket to prevent toothaches.
Medicinal: Soak hazelnuts in mead or honey water for coughs.
Culinary, Crafts: Hazelnuts are a popular ingredient in confections like cakes and custards. They add a lovely flavor to liqueurs, particularly when sweetened with honey, and can also be used to add texture to stir-fries.
Gardening, Habitat: Hazel trees thrive in well-drained soil, requiring little space.
Other: In the language of flowers, the hazel represents reconciliation.

Heather
Calluna spp.

Folk Names: None.
History: In the sixth century, Celts used heather flowers in brewing and for enhancing the flavor of honey. Devonshire's crest depicts a Dartmoor pony holding a heather sprig in its

mouth, and heather is the national flower of Scotland. Heather roots were once fashioned into musical pipes, while the foliage was used in mattress stuffing.

Folklore, Superstition, Magic: Bathing in water steeped with heather, particularly on May Day or during a full moon, increases beauty. In incense form, heather is said to bring rain. To safeguard against thievery and violence, carry a sprig in your purse or wallet. The ancients used heather as a classical folk cure for snakebites. The Scottish sleep on a bed of heather for health.

Medicinal: In aromatherapy, heather's aroma encourages peaceful outlooks, and a heather flower poultice eases aching joints.

Culinary, Crafts: Heather makes a lovely flavoring for meat and was also often used in brewing. To make a short heather ale, fill a good-sized non-aluminum pan with heather flowers and cover them with water. Note that organic dried heather will work for this recipe. Bring to a low rolling boil for an hour, then cool and strain. Measure the remaining liquid. To each gallon add a teaspoon of Cascade hops, a pint of sugar syrup, and half an inch of sliced, bruised ginger root. Warm until the syrup is dissolved before straining again. In a separate container, suspend half a package of beer yeast in warm water and put this in your gallon jug. Pour in the wine when lukewarm and leave it open to the air for twenty-four hours. Cork tightly and enjoy in two to three days. Note that since this is a short ale, it has a low alcohol content.

Other: None.

Hickory
Carya spp.

Folk Names: Ackroot, hickoria

History: Among the Algonquin and Creek peoples, hickory nuts were gathered for the winter months. They extracted the juices from both the nuts and shells to make a fermented drink and cooking oil from the nuts alone.

Folklore, Superstition, Magic: The groaning of a hickory tree portends a bad storm.

Carrying or decorating your home with hickory wood allays legal difficulties.

Culinary, Crafts: Of the twelve species that exist, shellbark hickory and pecan trees yield the most edible nuts. The nuts' milk was used in European cooking, especially to flavor venison and other game meats. If thickened with cornmeal, it can also be used to make bread or pancakes that are quite tasty.

Gardening, Habitat: Hickory grows slowly in damp soil.

Other: Hickory is an excellent burning wood that provides a bright flame. It's also prized for its strength and flexibility, making it ideal for construction. Try adding a few twigs on your grill for hickory-smoked meat.

───────

Honeysuckle
Lonicera caprifolium

Folk Names: Woodbine

History: Honeysuckle likely originated in China and Japan. The Japanese honeysuckle (*Lonicera japonica*) is one of the most well-known species and was introduced to North America in the nineteenth century.

Folklore, Superstition, Magic: If placed in a vase at home, honeysuckle attracts money. Grow honeysuckle near the home to bring luck. Placed over your doorways, honeysuckle keeps out fevers.

Medicinal: Chew on the plant's leaf to ease mouth sores. Use in an ointment to cool burns and bleach freckles. In Bach's flower remedies, honeysuckle is suggested as a remedial to help those who struggle with letting go of the past.

Culinary, Crafts: Honeysuckle makes a lovely wine that lives up to its name. Alternatively, honeysuckle syrup is another excellent option. Infuse two pounds of flowers in four pints of water for twelve hours, then extract the liquid and set it aside. Add twice the amount of sugar and cook until syrupy.

Gardening, Habitat: Honeysuckle can grow abundantly in various conditions, but it thrives best in sunny regions. Prune the older branches in spring after they shed their fruit to encourage this plant's growth.

Other: In the language of flowers, honeysuckle represents fraternal love.

Hops
Humulus lupulus

Folk Names: Bine, northern vine, beer flower
History: Hops have been grown for beer flavoring since the eleventh century and became increasingly popular in sixteenth-century England. It was originally used as a sedative. Hop pulp makes effective paper. The Swedes weave its fibers into fabric.
Folklore, Superstition, Magic: As an incense, hops bring sweet dreams and rejuvenation.
Medicinal: A hops infusion is a good stress reliever. For anxiety, try a tincture taken three to four times a day.
Culinary, Crafts: The ancient Romans ate young hop shoots like asparagus, cooking it until tender before seasoning. Make a sleepy-time pillow by combining hops with pine needles in a sachet. Slip the sachet in the center of your favorite

pillow's stuffing. The aroma reduces irritability and promotes a restful sleep.

Gardening, Habitat: Hops flourish along the roadsides of Europe and Asia. The flower is the most useful part, harvested in late summer or early fall and then dried.

Other: In the language of flowers, hops represent injustice.

───────

Horseradish
Armoracia rusticana

Folk Names: None.

History: Although horseradish is native to East Europe and West Asia, the Germans and the Danish were the only people during the Middle Ages who consumed horseradish on the dinner table; everyone else regarded it as a medicine! It didn't really gain popularity as a condiment in the United States until the mid-1800s.

Folklore, Superstition, Magic: Horseradish root sprinkled or planted around a home protects from evil influences. Pliny wrote that the root drives away scorpions.

Medicinal: Horseradish root has antibacterial properties and is high in vitamin C. When finely chopped and applied as a poultice, this root relieves aches and pains, especially on the neck. Horseradish tea is an effective way to prevent water retention. Take two to three tablespoons of it three times a day. Alternatively, eat a little on bread, add to salad with vinegar, or spread it over roast beef for similar effects. This has the additional benefit of alleviating hay fever.

Culinary, Crafts: Horseradish has a mustard-like flavor and may be used as a mustard substitute. The leaves are also edible as part of a salad. When pickling, add a little horseradish root to improve the crispness of your preparations. For a zesty cleansing and protective condiment, mix prepared horseradish with two tablespoons of sautéed, finely chopped onion, and an equal quantity of diced garlic. Remember to serve yourself and your guests a mint afterward!

Gardening, Habitat: This herb fares well in moist, well-drained, fertile soil. Space your plants twelve inches apart and consider companion-planting them with potatoes to deter potato bugs.

Other: Horseradish root stores better dry; when stored fresh, the root becomes bitter after a couple of months. Put a little into your bath if you're feeling particularly sluggish. In the Jewish seder, horseradish represents the bitterness of bondage.

Irish Moss

Chondrus crispus

Folk Names: Seaweed, pearl moss

History: Sea vegetables are used more in Asia than in the West where they are sometimes used for weight loss.

Folklore, Superstition, Magic: Wash the floors of an establishment with Irish moss to draw more customers. Place some beneath rugs and doorways for good luck and improved finances.

Medicinal: Apply it as a poultice to inflamed skin and drink it in tea to allay coughing or diarrhea.

Culinary, Crafts: Add Irish moss to your beer during the last half hour of boiling as a clarifier.

Gardening, Habitat: Irish moss is native to the coasts of Northern Europe and the United States. In Ireland, the plant is harvested in fall, while Americans harvest it in summer at low tide and then dry it in the sun.

Other: Irish moss is an additive in many foods and pharmaceutical items as a binding agent.

Jasmine
Jasminum officinale

Folk Names: Moonlight on the grove, jessamin
History: Jasmine was introduced to Europe in the sixteenth century, and jasmine tea has traditionally been used in Buddhist rituals.
Folklore, Superstition, Magic: To attract spiritual over physical love, wear jasmine perfume. Carry jasmine flowers as an effective charm for prosperity.
Medicinal: Put a few drops of jasmine oil in your bath to refresh and smooth your skin. To improve your sleep, rinse your linens in jasmine water, or apply the oil during a relaxing massage. Drink an infusion of flowers if you're having a restless night's sleep.
Culinary, Crafts: It takes four million handpicked flowers to make one pound of essential oil. In France, candied jasmine is a delicacy. It may be made into cakes and syrups or used to scent tea. For the latter, add a third cup of freshly dried petals to each cup of tea for a pleasant aroma.

To make a popular Italian liqueur, start by adding a quarter pound of fresh, clean blossoms to one liter of vodka. Steep the blossoms until they turn translucent, then strain. Next, dissolve one cup of honey in one cup of water and add to the base. Age for three months and then enjoy. This beverage continues to get better with age and may be blended with juices, more sweetener, and other spices to taste.
Gardening, Habitat: Native to India and the Himalayas, jasmine may be cultivated as a garden plant in warm regions where the soil is rich and loamy.

Other: In the language of flowers, the white jasmine represents a friendly nature, while the yellow symbolizes poise and refinement. In aromatherapy, jasmine is recommended for stress, depression, and anxiety attacks.

Juniper
Juniperus communis

Folk Names: Gin berry, geneva

History: Juniper takes its name from the Dutch *jenever,* which is also the origin for the modern beverage gin. The berries from some species of this tree are used to make gin. The Native Americans put the western variety of this to good use, weaving mats and cloth from thin strips of bark.

Folklore, Superstition, Magic: Grow junipers around your home to keep it safe from thieves, ghosts, and other malevolent influences. In Italian homes, juniper was placed over the doorway to keep out witches. Carrying juniper keeps you hearty, and as an incense, it banishes negativity and improves psychic awareness. Juniper's shade, however, is not a good influence on crops or animals.

Medicinal: Juniper berries and leaves in a poultice may be applied to the skin for bruises and sore muscles. The berries when eaten decrease gas, coughing, and cramping. As a cream, juniper eases hemorrhoids and dermatitis. The berries are high in vitamin C. Do not use this herb when pregnant, as it can stimulate menstruation.

Culinary, Crafts: Native Americans and early colonial settlers both enjoyed eating the tree's fruit. Today, small amounts of juniper flowers and berries make lovely additions to a salad and as a pre-seasoning for game meats when mixed frugally into pâté. When cooking, try placing tiny juniper branches in your grill's coals to give meats a unique flavor. As a substitute, use four juniper berries in place of one bay leaf.

Gardening, Habitat: Juniper prefers gravel-laden, dry soil. The fruit is harvested in the fall when ripe.

Other: If a region is prone to harsh windstorms, juniper— particularly the dwarf variety—serves as a good windbreaker. Red juniper is a species commonly used to make pencils. Juniper's aroma stimulates and revitalizes energy. In the language of flowers, juniper represents asylum.

Lavender
Lavandula officinale

Folk Names: Spike, elf leaf

History: This was a favorite flower for strewing on floors alongside roses to bring aroma and beauty to a room containing honored guests. In Roman times, it was commonly used in bathhouses. Lavender was cultivated for medicinal purposes as early as 1568 CE.

Folklore, Superstition, Magic: According to Christian legend, this herb originally had no aroma. The herb gained its pleasing scent after Mary dried baby Jesus's clothing on a lavender bush. Wear a sprig of lavender near your head to avert colds through the winter. If put in a pouch, this herb safeguards the bearer from cruel treatment by a spouse. Lay your sight upon these flowers to lift your spirits and smell their lovely aroma to secure a long life. Place lavender under your pillow and make a wish. If you dream of your wish, it will come true.

Medicinal: Take distilled water from lavender and mix it in equal quantities with honey. This effectively soothes sore throats and coughs. For headaches, Parkinson recommended the herb for relief. As an aroma, lavender offsets headaches, tension, and insomnia.

Culinary, Crafts: Lavender flavors many sweets, specifically conserves. To make this, mix one part flowers to three parts sugar and add a little water until the mixture thickens. The conserves have a shelf life of one year. For a subtler sweetness, include lavender in tea or wine. Lavender can also be pickled for future use. Mix the flowers, vinegar, and sugar in equal parts, then store in an airtight container.

Gardening, Habitat: Lavender prefers a sunny spot in the garden and fares best in warmer climates with lime-laden, dry soil and plenty of light. Harvest the flowers in midsummer and protect the plants in winter using mulch.

Other: Include sweet bags filled with lavender in chests and cupboards to prevent insect infestation. Lavender oil mixed with beeswax makes a serviceable, sweet-smelling furniture polish. In the language of flowers, lavender represents acknowledgment.

Lemon
Citrus limonum

Folk Names: Limon

History: The lemon originates from India and found its way to Europe around 2 CE. It was a popular dental aid for sailors during the 1400s as it prevented scurvy. Casanova mentions the use of both the juice and the rind as a contraceptive in the Balkans.

Folklore, Superstition, Magic: The scent and flavor of lemon is said to improve passion, adoration, and friendship. During the Middle Ages, cloved lemons were exchanged for a kiss. If the gift was accepted, the romantic interest was mutual. Italian magicians sometimes use lemons as an alternative poppet for spellcasting.

Medicinal: As a fruit rich in vitamin C, lemon strengthens the immune system. Practically, lemon juice or dried rind is a good additive for cold teas or as part of a gargle for sore throats. Lemon oil helps dry canker and cold sores when mixed with water in a one-to-five ratio.

Culinary, Crafts: Both the fruit and flowers of this tree are edible. Use lemon blossoms in ice cream, jam, butter, tarts, and pudding. For a unique salad dressing, mix lemon flower water with two cups of vinegar and four to five tablespoons of honey to taste. A Greek lemon sauce, excellent for flavoring chicken and asparagus, is prepared by beating two egg yolks while slowly adding the juice from half a lemon. Slowly add half a cup of warm chicken broth and cook over a double boiler for seven minutes. Optionally, add salt, pepper, garlic, and a hint of honey to taste before serving with your chosen meat or vegetable.

Gardening, Habitat: Lemon trees need plenty of direct sunlight and well-drained soil. They are very sensitive to frost and accustomed to Mediterranean climates. Harvest the fruit in winter for the highest amount of vitamin C to be present.

Other: Around the house, lemon juice is a mild antiseptic that offers a natural cleaning solution for the home. Add a little to your wash water for clothes or floors for a lovely scent and to effectively combat germs. In the language of flowers, lemon blossoms represent meekness and discretion.

Licorice
Glycyrrhiza glabra

Folk Names: Sweet root, black sugar, Spanish juice, lick weed (Jamaica), Scythian root (Greece)

History: Since the times of Alexander the Great, people have chewed the root, using it as a candy and a thirst quencher. Settlers considered licorice a precious herb and brought it with them to North America.

Folklore, Superstition, Magic: The *Kama Sutra* recommends licorice mingled with milk and sweetener as an aphrodisiac.

Medicinal: The ancient Greeks recommended licorice for colds and mouth sores. Today, herbalists suggest a tincture or chewing on a dried juice stick for an acidic stomach, a licorice decoction for constipation, and a powder for canker sores. Do not use licorice when pregnant.

Culinary, Crafts: Perhaps best known for flavoring candy, licorice is also valuable to brewers as it provides a good heady foam for stouts.

Gardening, Habitat: Licorice grows in temperate regions in Europe and southwest Asia. The roots are harvested at maturity (about four years) during the fall. It prefers wet clay soils.

Other: Add licorice to facial steams to open the pores. It also makes an excellent rinse for oily hair.

———————

Lilac
Syringa vulgaris

History: Lilac was introduced Europe in 1597 by way of Vienna, possibly originating in Persia. It derives its name from a Greek word meaning *pipe* or *reed*. George Washington planted the first lilac tree at Mount Vernon.

Folklore, Superstition, Magic: Scottish legend says that the first lilac seeds were dropped by a falcon into an old woman's garden. The bush did not blossom until a young prince's plume dropped on it, yielding purple blossoms. Plant lilac around your home to keep it safe from wandering spirits, but do not bring the blossoms into the house—this is unlucky. Use lilac oil as an aromatic in your home to decrease negativity. Bathe in lilac water on May Day to capture beauty for an entire year.

Culinary, Crafts: Lilacs may be candied in gum arabic, corn syrup, and sugar. Add the candied flowers to marzipan.

Gardening, Habitat: Lilac prefers a lime-rich soil with higher acidity. It should not be crowded in the garden. For hardier growth, deflower the bushes before they produce seed.

Other: Purple lilacs represent first love, while white ones symbolize youthful happiness. In the language of flowers, lilac represents meticulousness.

Lily
Lilium spp.

Folk Names: The Lily of Faith (Dante), meadow lily
History: The Chinese consider lilies the flower of forgetfulness. In classical art, St. Dominic holds a lily.
Folklore, Superstition, Magic: Legend says that lilies blossomed from Eve's tears when she was expelled from the Garden of Eden. English superstition says that smelling lilies gives you freckles. Because of its white color and beauty, the lily is sacred to many of the world's goddesses and consequently has come to symbolize purity.
Medicinal: In antiquity, lily roots were ground with honey and applied to torn muscles or mixed with oil to ease aching muscles and condition hair. Apply bruised leaves to swellings or apply the juice for itchy bug bites.
Culinary, Crafts: In Asia, where the lily is a popular edible flower, pork is sometimes cooked with dried lily blossoms, as are some soups and noodle dishes.
Gardening, Habitat: Plant bulbs deeply into porous, graveled loam for good drainage. Fertilize with old leaves, grass, and compost.
Other: In the language of flowers, this represents beauty. Christianity associates the lily with Christ and thus with purity. The ancient Chinese, Japanese, Indians, and Egyptians viewed it as a symbol of fertility.

Lotus
Nymphaea lotus

Folk Names: Flower of light, tropical water lily, fairest flower

History: In China, some people believe this was the first flower to appear on Earth. Ancient Egyptians decorated bottles of wine and beer with the image of a lotus, and some people wore the flowers to entice others.

Folklore, Superstition, Magic: In some Buddhist traditions, the lotus represents fertility and life's cycles, specifically life, death, and rebirth into a better, more divine existence. This may be why the energy centers known as chakras, which are believed to affect health and psychic abilities, are often depicted as lotuses in Eastern art.

In both Egyptian and Greco-Roman traditions, this became associated with the goddess as lotus-born, in an odd dichotomy of fecundity and virginity. Buddhists identify the lotus with the wheel of life, and depictions include lotus petals on the wheel's rim. In this tradition, a soul reborn into paradise arrives on a lotus leaf.

Wearing lotus is auspicious, carrying it attracts health, and when found in odd locations or seen in a dream, it portends improvements in relationships.

Medicinal: The plant's rhizome in a decoction is an ancient cure for digestive troubles, especially those affecting the intestines.

Culinary, Crafts: In East Asia, nearly every part of the lotus is used in the kitchen, including the tubers for vegetables and candies, the stems for making arrowroot, and the kernels for soup or for snacking in roasted form. In 500 BCE, the historian Herodotus noted that the Egyptians used lotus in baking bread.

Gardening, Habitat: Lotus prefers sunny, sheltered ponds where it is protected from cold winds.

Other: In the language of flowers, the lotus represents distant love.

Magnolia
Magnolia officinalis

Folk Names: Cucumber tree, white bay, beaver tree, sweet magnolia

History: The Chinese propagated white magnolia as early as 627 CE, and it was a gift considered suitable for an emperor.

Folklore, Superstition, Magic: Lovers recited vows under or near a blossoming magnolia tree to ensure fidelity in their relationship.

Medicinal: Known as *hou po* in China, magnolia bark is used to relax muscles since approximately the first century CE.

Culinary, Crafts: These flowers make a lovely aromatic addition to scented oils, incense, and potpourri.

Gardening, Habitat: Magnolia is native to China and grows wild in mountain regions. It is frequently cultivated for landscaping in warmer regions. It requires deep, fertile soil, indirect sunlight, and protection from harsh winds.

Other: In the language of flowers, it represents a love of nature or splendor. In earlier times, the bark of this tree was sometimes used as a substitute for chewing tobacco.

Mandrake
Mandragora officinarum

Folk Names: *Galgen-mannlein* (Old Germanic), Circe's plant, devil's candle (Saudi Arabia), Satan's testicles, dragon doll, fool's apple

History: Romans treated "insanity" with mandrake root, while the Greeks applied it as an anesthetic during surgery.

Folklore, Superstition, Magic: European folk traditions say this plant screams when pulled from the ground and only grows under gallows. Because the root bears a humanlike form, magicians often carved it for spells or made talismans to protect against trouble, provide invulnerability, reveal treasure, or improve fertility.

Mandrake also had associations with Aphrodite and consequently was used in love potions with wine. To this day, some young people in Greece carry bits of root as a love charm.
Medicinal: Due to the plant's toxicity, mandrake is strictly applied externally, such as a poultice for skin disorders and joint pains. It should be kept in unbreakable containers that are well out of the reach of pets and children.
Gardening, Habitat: Mandrake prefers low, shady areas with rich, deep soil. The root is collected in late October after the first fruits ripen.
Other: In the language of flowers, mandrake represents horror.

Marigold
Tagetes erecta

Folk Names: Holigold, ruddles, summer's bride, solsequia, *elois* (Chaldea), *eliotropium* (Latin regions), calendula, jack-anapes-on-horsebacke (Gerald)
History: Marigold is sacred in India, adorning many Hindu temples. Gerald noted marigolds are used in Dutch cuisine, particularly in soup. According to a Mexican myth, these flowers sprang from the blood of those slain during Cortez's conquest.
Folklore, Superstition, Magic: In 1560, Albertus Magnus recommended harvesting this flower when the sun is in Leo—typically in August—and suggested bundling it with a bay leaf and a wolf's tooth to allay gossip.

When plucked at noon, this flower brings comfort to the bearer. Garlands of marigolds in the home will protect the residents from evil. Placing marigolds beneath one's bed invites prophetic dreams, and bathing in marigold water assures admiration from others. A person walking over this flower will understand the birds and, in some traditions, see fairies.

Medicinal: A marigold rinse tones the skin and brings out hair highlights. As a lotion, it eases itching, and as a tea, it relieves cramps and flu symptoms. Some say soaking in bathwater strewn with marigolds shrinks varicose veins.

Culinary, Crafts: In German kitchens, marigolds found their way into various dishes, including eggs, soups, breads, and conserves. With their tangy flavor, the flower enhances the taste of the following light, low-calorie rice dish for two. Mix half a teaspoon of marigold petals with a half cup of chicken broth, one cup of cooked rice, two tablespoons of cooked onion, half a pound of baby shrimp, and cheese of your choice.

Gardening, Habitat: Marigolds are easy to grow in the garden, tolerating shade, sun, and diverse soil conditions. Do not sow them until the threat of frost has passed.

Other: In the Middle Ages, this flower symbolized jealousy. Later in France, it came to symbolize worry, while in Mexico it denoted death. Marigold also represents grief, sorrow, and burdens in the language of flowers. Observe marigolds early in the morning to forecast the weather; if they do not open by seven, it will rain or thunder.

Marjoram
Origanum majorana

Folk Names: Joy of the mountains, mountain mint, wintersweet, herb of grace (Shakespeare)

History: Marjoram is native to north Africa and Southwest Asia. The Greeks used it to remedy rheumatism and wore it at weddings. This is not surprising since the herb was sacred to Aphrodite, the Greek goddess of love. Aristotle wrote that tortoises eat marjoram after swallowing a snake to save their life. Gerard recommended the herb to combat bouts of sighing.

Folklore, Superstition, Magic: Many ancient civilizations regarded this herb as sacred to the gods, including Osiris in Egypt and Vishnu in India. The Romans planted the herb on grave sites to ensure a restful spirit.

In Germany, marjoram keeps witches, ghosts, and goblins away. Its name comes from the Greek words *oros gams,* which mean "mountain joy." It is believed to have been given this name because it improves one's spirits. Marjoram was used frequently in love spells and potions during the Middle Ages. The aroma of marjoram also improves mental keenness.

Medicinal: Wild marjoram is the most common herb in folk medicine. Marjoram, fresh or as a tea, eases indigestion and tackles insomnia. The tea, consumed or even gargled, can also alleviate hay fever and asthma. Use its oil to relieve swelling or sore joints.

To make a fast salve, take a small jar of petroleum jelly or cold cream. Warm it slowly over a low flame and steep a cup full of marjoram. Once the jelly or cream has a heady scent, remove the plant pieces and beat the cream until cool. Return the jelly or cream to its original container, close the lid tightly, and use as desired.

Culinary, Crafts: In the pantry, sweet marjoram is used mostly for pork, veal, and liver. It is also a wonderful addition to soups, stews, and salads. If you are running short on oregano, marjoram is a perfect substitute with a similar taste (and vice versa).

Gardening, Habitat: Marjoram fares best in cool, wet regions, but the wild variety, *Origanum vulgare,* is hardier and tolerates a variety of soil conditions. Both types need partial shade for best growth.

Other: In the Middle Ages, marjoram was frequently strewed for its scent, making it a valuable addition to sachets, sweet bags, finger water, and potpourri blends. Rinsing your face with marjoram water can be beneficial to your complexion.

Marsh Mallow
Althaea officinalis

Folk Names: Sweet weed, witte malve, mallards, mortification root

History: Galen and Dioscorides reference marsh mallow, a plant native to Europe, as a constituent in wines made to alleviate coughs. Pliny states that the mallow was so highly valuable for its medicinal properties that it was dug with a golden tool. The herb was also favored in the Middle Ages to ease swelling and combat constipation.

Folklore, Superstition, Magic: Marsh mallow was frequently used for protection during the Middle Ages. When carried, the plant's leaves were regarded as a protective amulet, while the root could be boiled with raisins and consumed in the morning to protect against all maladies.

Ointments made from marsh mallow protect a wearer from bewitchment or break its effects.

Medicinal: Marsh mallow root is a mild laxative that alleviates many digestive issues. You can also make the root into an ointment for boils or create a tincture for a mouth rinse. An infusion of the leaves is good for congestion, while the flowers can soothe itching skin.

Culinary, Crafts: Originally, marshmallows were (unsurprisingly) made from this plant but have since been replaced by gelatin. Marsh mallow flowers still make a good tea or syrup additive. The French sauté the roots with onions, herbs, and butter or olive oil.
Gardening, Habitat: Marsh mallow, as the name implies, likes marshy regions. Its flowers and leaves are harvested in summer, and the roots are harvested in fall.

Peeled marsh mallow root is a good teething toy for babies. In the language of flowers, it represents mildness.

Meadowsweet
Filipendula ulmaria

Folk Names: Queen of the meadow, meadwort, bridewort, lady-of-the-meadow, maid of the meadow, trumpet weed, gravel root, steeplebush, silver rushes (Ireland)
History: In the 1500s, Gerald wrote meadowsweet makes hearts merry, which perhaps explains why it was a favorite strewing herb during the Middle Ages. The Irish sometimes used this plant as a scouring implement.
Folklore, Superstition, Magic: Welsh legend says that meadowsweet was one of the flowers used to create Blodeuwedd, the petaled wife to Llew. Meadowsweet participated in love magic and spells to discern the identity of a thief. When tension rises at home, bring meadowsweet indoors; its soothing aroma brings peace.
Medicinal: Culpeper recommended meadowsweet mixed with wine to treat an upset stomach, a practice still deemed safe. An infusion of meadowsweet aids diarrhea, while a tincture soothes sore joints.

Culinary, Crafts: Meadowsweet has a versatile, mild almond flavor. Use meadowsweet leaves in tea or to flavor soup. For a refreshing twist, combine with raspberry leaves to flavor beers and other cold summer beverages. To do this, you can make a syrup and dilute as needed.

Gardening, Habitat: Meadowsweet is native to Europe and grows readily in damp areas. The flowers and leaves are usually harvested in midsummer.

Other: In the language of flowers, this represents uselessness.

Mint
Mentha spp.

Folk Names: Garden mint, heart mint, lamb mint, hairy mint, mackerel mint

History: Mint, native to Europe and Asia, held various cultural significances throughout history. In ancient times, the Pharisees reportedly used it as a tithe. Pliny recommended its scent for uplifting spirits. Both ancient Hebrews and Greeks incorporated mint regularly in rituals and used it as a strewing herb in temples. The Greeks also made perfume from it.

Pliny recommended wreathing one's head with mint before studying, while Hippocrates and Aristotle warned of impotence. In the Middle Ages, pennyroyal was used to repel fleas, while other types of mint were added to bathwater for calming nerves and soothing sore muscles. In the 1500s, a potion made from mint, vervain, and wormwood was used to combat hydrophobia.

Folklore, Superstition, Magic: In Greek mythology, Minthe, a nymph beloved by Hades, was transformed into a fragrant plant by Persephone, Hades' wife, out of jealousy. The Greeks believed mint was a symbol of hospitality but also thought it could reduce courage and therefore forbade warriors from eating it. Contrary to Hippocrates' claim, the Arabs believed mint improves virility. Mint protects from sickness when worn and ensures safety when kept in the home. Discovering a blossoming mint on St. John's Day predicts a lifetime of joy for the lucky finder.

Medicinal: Mint was not prominent in medicine until the 1700s but was very popular as a tea in colonial America because it wasn't taxed like other varieties! As it became more widely embraced in medicine, mint tea was used to ease gas, diarrhea, and mild digestive disorders. It was and is also recommended for migraines, to improve sleep, and to calm the nerves. A great old remedy for stomach cramps includes a cup of warm milk steeped with a few fresh mint leaves (peppermint is the best choice). This drink can also curtail hunger for a few hours.

The best part about mint is that it is perfectly safe. The next time you have a headache, crush some fresh leaves and apply them to your temples and forehead. For chapped hands, wash them with spearmint water.

Culinary, Crafts: Sprinkle finely chopped mint mixed with sugar. To add a subtle flavor to potatoes, add a single fresh mint leaf between each slice before baking them in the oven or grilling.

Combine two teaspoons of finely chopped fresh mint with a quarter cup of olive oil, minced garlic to taste, three sliced cucumbers, salt, and two tablespoons of wine vinegar. Mix all ingredients thoroughly. Add some diced chives as a garnish, if desired. This makes for a refreshing side dish.

Try this recipe for a great jelly that also tastes delicious on ice cream. Place seven cups of chopped apples in a large pot with just enough water to cover them. Boil this until the fruit is tender (about forty minutes). Mash this until smooth, then let the mixture strain out overnight so the juices drain into a separate container. Set the fruit aside and use it for applesauce later. Pour the juice back into your pan, adding one cup of sugar for every cup of juice. Heat this until the sugar is well incorporated, then boil until the jelly stage is reached on a thermometer, typically eight degrees higher than the boiling point.

Meanwhile, in five half-pint jars, place one-eighth cup of each finely chopped apple mint and pineapple mint leaves. Fill the jars with the sugar liquid, seal, and process in a boiling water bath for eight to ten minutes. Check for a good seal on the jars before storing them for use.

For best results, always use fresh young mint leaves, harvested before the heat of the day. Older ones tend to be tart.

Gardening, Habitat: Mint grows well in shady, damp areas; in fact, it grows a bit too well! Only cultivate this plant if you want *a lot*, or balance it with parsley to deter its abundant growth. Harvest it before flowering during dry, sunny weather.

Other: Mint water, chilled like a tea, makes an effective mouthwash. Mint is effective to keep your home pest-free. Leave dried mint leaves in drawers to repel moths and fleas. Placing fresh mint leaves on your picnic table can help keep ants away. In the language of flowers, it represents virtue. This is rather amusing, given that the herbalist Culpeper says that mint stirs up bodily lust! Finally, grow or place mint around your home to keep mice at bay.

Mistletoe
Viscum album

Folk Names: Golden bough, all heal, birdlime, Devil's fuge

History: According to Pliny, druids picked mistletoe on the sixth day of the moon using only a golden sickle. After harvesting, they would offer a ritual of sacrifice to the tree as a gesture of gratitude. Mistletoe was an herb of immortality because it was an evergreen plant.

Folklore, Superstition, Magic: Ancient people believed that mistletoe could cure many ills such as ulcers, infertility, and poison. The Japanese considered mistletoe from a willow tree the most potent.

Mistletoe is widely believed to offer protection. People in some parts of Africa carried mistletoe to protect against evil magic, while the Swedish used it to ward off trolls. The Italians and Scandinavians felt mistletoe properly harvested could put out fires and protect their homes from lightning strikes. The Welsh considered it an herb of good fortune.

If a person carries mistletoe found growing on a hazel tree, they will discover hidden treasures. Divining rods cut from mistletoe on Midsummer Day are also considered more effective.

Medicinal: A cup of a mistletoe infusion before meals may help with high blood pressure and migraines. Due to the herb's toxicity in larger quantities, it should be prepared by an expert. Researchers are currently investigating mistletoe as a potential combatant for cancer.

Culinary, Crafts: During the holidays, place a sprig in doorways or mid-ceiling and sneak a kiss from a sweetheart.

Gardening, Habitat: Despite its association with oak trees, this plant grows more readily on apple or pear trees. It is typically harvested in October or November when the berries mature, and the leaves are used for remedial purposes.

Other: Do not use this herb during pregnancy, as it is potentially toxic. In the language of flowers, this represents overcoming obstacles and difficulties.

Mugwort
Artemisia vulgaris

Folk Names: Felon herb, artemisia, St. John's plant, old man, lad's love, southernwood, *garderole* (France)

History: Sometimes regarded as a symbol of forgetfulness, mugwort was a popular flavoring in beer until it was replaced by hops. In Europe, it was often used as a border plant in castle gardens.

Folklore, Superstition, Magic: The folk name, *artemisia,* derives from Artemis, the Greek goddess of the hunt. Romans placed mugwort in their shoes to promote healthy feet, and in thirteenth-century Wales, people bound it to their left thigh for fertility.

The Anglo-Saxons favored mugwort to protect against both fatigue and evil influences. Sleeping on a mugwort pillow brings prophetic dreams and hanging the plant in one's house wards off lightning strikes.

Finally, place mugwort in your shoes when walking long distances to improve stamina.

Medicinal: Mugwort flower tea manages irregular menstrual cycles and is a good tea additive for bronchitis. Do not use it during pregnancy, as it induces menstruation. Chinese acupuncture uses mugwort in some treatments. Add some to herb baths to soothe aches or stuff a pillow with mugwort to ensure a good night's rest and vivid dreams.

Culinary, Crafts: In France, chefs sometimes use the young shoots of *Artemisia abrotanum* to add flavor to cakes and other foods.

Gardening, Habitat: Mugwort is a relative of wormwood. It grows in temperate regions and takes well to both the garden and roadside. Harvest it in late summer before it flowers.

Other: Mugwort's sage-lemon scent discourages bees and other insects. Place some leaves in your clothes to deter moths.

───────

Mulberry
Moms rubra

Folk Names: Redberry
History: This tree was first cultivated in China in 2700 BCE, not for its fruit, but to feed silkworms! The Greeks also grew mulberry for this reason, beginning around 350 BCE. Mulberry was so strongly associated with silk production that it became a heraldic symbol identifying silk makers in the Middle Ages.
Folklore, Superstition, Magic: In Rome, mulberries were sacred to Minerva. In the Bible, God sent a sign to David in the form of a rustling mulberry tree. The great herbalist

Pliny believed these trees exhibited prudence and patience because they waited until long after winter to bear leaves. Generally, mulberry bushes are believed to protect from lightning and evildoers.

Medicinal: Mulberry was a sympathetic cure based on the doctrine of signatures during the Middle Ages. Because of its crimson color, mulberry was believed to cure "red-related" illnesses and used to treat blood disorders.

Mulberry tea is good for menstrual difficulties, and mulberry juice will help treat canker sores. The leaves, when bruised with vinegar and applied as a poultice, can ease mild burns. The root boiled in vinegar relieves toothache, and the leaves themselves can be applied to minor cuts and scrapes akin to a bandage.

Culinary, Crafts: Mulberry branch nodes taste sweet when chewed. However, the berries, which ripen between July and August, are generally preferred for making pies, tarts, and beverages.

Gardening, Habitat: Mulberry is native to both Europe and Asia and grows wild in the United States. If your garden contains any fruit that you wish to keep safe from birds, grow a few mulberry bushes. The birds will eat the fruits of these bushes instead.

Other: The base fibers from mulberry bark make good ropes and coarse fabric cloths. The berries are said to be healthy for pigs and game birds. Once the mulberry begins to show leaves, there should be no more frost.

Mustard
Brassica spp.

Folk Names: Golden mustard, Chinese mustard, southern curled
History: Mustard is a member of the cress family, which includes horseradish, cauliflower, and cabbage. It is mentioned in the Bible, and the Greeks regularly wrote about its flavor

and usefulness in medicine. Romans used wine with mustard seed as an earlier version of the modern condiment. By the seventh century, wine mustard was readily available in France, which became the main source for all of Europe.

Folklore, Superstition, Magic: Carrying mustard seeds will keep colds away and increase conscious self-awareness. Bury mustard under your doorstep for protection. The mustard seed, being small but very potent, symbolizes faith.

In Hindu tradition, mustard allows the bearer to magically travel through the air and discover secret places, possibly alluding to astral projection. In Greece, people believed consuming mustard seed mixed with honey would prevent pregnancy.

Medicinal: Mustard essence is believed to promote cheerfulness and serenity in one of *Bach's Flower Essences'* homeopathic products.

Mustard plaster—a mixture of mustard seed and vinegar applied to the skin—is commonly used to alleviate irritation, swelling, and congestion. The plaster should not be left on the skin for more than thirty minutes. If you have sensitive skin, add an egg white to the mixture and test it on a small area first. Rinse the skin carefully afterward.

An old Native American cure for sore joints consisted of mixing black mustard seeds with fat and rubbing them into the joints. You can make something similar by mixing one tablespoon of crushed black mustard seeds with a quarter cup of shortening and simmering it over a low flame. Pour the liquid into an airtight container and allow it to re-solidify, then apply as needed.

Culinary, Crafts: Gather mustard greens early in the spring and enjoy them raw in salads, or cook them with other vegetables, adding butter and salt. They are very high in vitamins.

To make your own table mustard, follow this recipe:

- ⅓ cup wine vinegar
- ⅔ cup wine
- 2 tbsp honey
- ⅓ tsp salt

- ⅓ cup brown mustard seeds
- 1 tbsp olive oil

Boil the wine vinegar, wine, honey, and salt together. While hot, add the mustard seeds, then move the entire mixture to a blender. Grind until smooth, slowly adding olive oil. Store this mixture in an airtight container in the refrigerator unless canned afterward.

This makes about one cup and a half of zesty mustard. For a flavorful surprise, add one tablespoon of finely chopped garlic during the boiling process.

Gardening, Habitat: Plant mustard in rows twelve inches apart. Gather the young plants for a salad at about four inches high and for a vegetable green at six inches high. If the summer is particularly hot, either flavor may be too strong, but the seed can still be gathered to make condiments.

Other: Dry mustard mixed with lemon juice helps remove freckles. Apply this for four successive nights.

Myrrh
Commiphora molmol

Folk Names: Myrrha

History: Probably best known as the herb the Magus of Persia brought to Christ's birth, myrrh was used in numerous ancient civilizations for religious purposes. It was an element of embalming fluids and part of the incense offered to the gods in Egypt. In the Old Testament, Moses instructed the priests to anoint themselves with myrrh.

Folklore, Superstition, Magic: In Greek mythology, Aphrodite bewitched a princess named Myrrha into having intercourse with her own father. To escape death by her father's hand, she was transformed by the gods into a myrrh tree. The drops of this tree's sap are said to be Myrrha's tears.

Medicinal: A myrrh tincture or gargle can treat canker sores and bleeding gums. Alternatively, use this as a wash to clear up skin problems like acne. In Ayurvedic medicine, myrrh tonic promotes passion and purifies the system.

Culinary, Crafts: Myrrh powder is a powerful aromatic that may be added to homemade incense, oils, soaps, and perfumes. As a bonus, the aroma repels mosquitoes.

Gardening, Habitat: Myrrh thrives best in hot regions like India, Africa, and Saudi Arabia. In these climates, people cultivate the tree in spring and gather the resin from trimmed branches.

Other: Vets sometimes use myrrh as an unguent for animal wounds.

———

Nasturtium
Tropaeolum majus

Folk Names: None.

History: Native to Peru, nasturtium migrated around the world with Spanish conquistadors. Dwight D. Eisenhower liked boiled nasturtium stems in his soup.

Folklore, Superstition, Magic: Carry the bright red flowers for energy and luck.

Medicinal: Nasturtium is high in vitamin C and contains natural antiseptic qualities. As a tea, it aids digestion, allays chest trouble, and makes an effective overall tonic.

Culinary, Crafts: Nasturtium flowers and leaves are edible and have a peppery taste. In a salad, mix them with grated orange rind, lemon balm, shallots, chives, orange juice, and wine vinegar. Add the petals to a vegetable soup or stuff them in a salad for a beautiful serving bowl. Chop the tops and mix them with cream cheese or butter for breads, or use seeds like capers to spice things up.

Gardening, Habitat: Nasturtiums fare well in poor soil, especially if planted on the north side of the house. Do not plant them near tomatoes or peppers; they have common bacterial enemies. Instead, sow nasturtium near cabbage and squash to keep bugs away from those vegetables.

Other: Steep them in water, then rinse your scalp with the tincture after shampooing to keep the scalp clean. In the language of flowers, nasturtium may represent either conquest or patriotism.

Nettle
Urtica dioica

Folk Names: Stinging nettle

History: Dioscorides noted various applications of nettle, such as using the leaves for cleaning septic wounds and its juice for stanching nosebleeds. Pliny purportedly loved nettle pudding, and Gerald advocated eating nettle baked with sugar to ensure vitality. In *Les Misérables*, Victor Hugo recounts the use of nettle as fodder and in making canvas and dye.

Folklore, Superstition, Magic: Since nettle was sacred to Thor, wearing it became a badge of courage. Germans believed nettle gathered in the wee hours of the morning would cure sick cattle. They also considered nettle an aphrodisiac.

In magical traditions, the herb is sometimes used to dispel curses. Nettle around the house wards against negativity and acts as a protective amulet when carried.

Medicinal: Nettle has been a commonly used medicinal herb throughout history. The Romans made it into cold ointments, while the Irish used it to treat consumption, and some Native American tribes favored nettle in preparations for urinary disorders.

Use nettle ointment for itchy skin, the juice to regulate heavy menstruation, and the root as a diuretic.

Culinary, Crafts: Nettle has a flavor akin to spinach and is a good additive to carrot soup. This has the extra benefit of acting as an iron tonic.

To make nettle beer, gather one gallon of nettle tops, two pounds of malt, one gallon of water, one ounce of hops, two ounces of other herbs (your choice), a slice of lemon, half an ounce of pineapple mint, and three-quarters pound of sugar. Warm this over a low flame until the sugar dissolves. Strain the blend when cool, add yeast (see Chapter Two), and age.

Gardening, Habitat: Nettle grows well in all northern temperate regions, requiring very little fuss. Harvest the shoots in spring for vegetables, the leaves in summer, and the roots in fall.

Other: Nettle can be used as a dye, mixed with alum for a yellow-green hue or with chrome for tan coloration. In the language of flowers, it represents slander.

Nutmeg
Myristica fragrans

Folk Names: Jaiphal

History: Nutmeg is among the oldest spices known to humankind. One of the first written records of its use comes from the Persian philosopher Avicenna around 1000 CE. It is a native of the Spice Islands and a member of the snapdragon family.

Romans scattered nutmeg on the streets during some festival days. During the Middle Ages, healers used it as part of Europe and India's costly medicinal liqueurs and remedials. It also appeared regularly in French love potions. The shell of the nutmeg yields another spice, mace.

Folklore, Superstition, Magic: Nutmeg has often been associated with psychic experiences. The outer shell, when carried, is said to increase psychic visions, and ingesting the nut has been connected to religious visions, although the practice is considered unsafe. During the Victorian era, some people placed nutmeg in a silver garter to bring sleep. In Saudi Arabia and India, people regard nutmeg as an aphrodisiac.

Medicinal: In the doctrine of signatures, nutmeg is believed to cure brain illnesses because it resembles that organ. Some people believed that carrying nutmeg prevented other ailments, including loss of vision.

Nutmeg is an effective aid to digestion and circulation when used in careful moderation (no more than what is used for culinary purposes). It can be added to tea or coffee or consumed as part of a mildly spiced bread.

Culinary, Crafts: Nutmeg is used regularly as a beverage garnish and as a flavoring for various meats and desserts, especially pies and cookies. Probably the most popular beverage that adds nutmeg is eggnog. Now that supermarkets carry pre-prepared eggnog, dressing the mixture up with a dab of whipped cream and a sprinkling of nutmeg is easy.

Gardening, Habitat: The tree bearing nutmeg is native to the East Indies and prefers seaside locations. It produces about 1,500 to 2,000 nuts a year.

Other: Nutmeg beads can be used for craft projects, specifically all-natural wind chimes. To make one, string them in lines around a wooden base together with dried fruit rinds and a clapper before hanging it by a warm window. The chime also acts as an air freshener, and it mystically prevents boils, cold sores, and sties if hung around the neck. Add nutmeg to your household wash water for a wonderful scent.

Oak
Quercus alba

Folk Names: Tanner's bark, strong oak
History: In ancient Greece, priests of Zeus would interpret rustling oak leaves for prophetic messages. Oak was sacred to various peoples of antiquity, including the Hebrews, Teutons,

Romans, and Celts. According to legend, it was under the great bows of an oak that Joan of Arc first heard the voices of angels. Shrines for many ancient kings were carved from this wood, as was the traditional Yule log. The Romans crowned honored guests, heroes, and winners of competitions with a wreath of oak leaves. Strabo (55 BCE–25 CE) reports that the Galatian senate would convene among oak trees.

Folklore, Superstition, Magic: In Greece, people believed the dryads were spirits of the oak, and the druids conducted rituals in oak groves. Oak ashes were believed to heal the land and improve crops when mixed into the soil because of their strong, hardy nature.

Legends tell us that Merlin worked magic for King Arthur under an oak's branches, while the Bible recounts Abraham meeting with angels by the tree. In Scandinavia, coming across an oak struck by lightning foretells disaster. Weather lore says that if an oak's leaves open before those of an ash, rain will be light in the coming season.

Eating acorns, the fruit of the oak, ensures longevity. Carrying acorns aids fertility and protects the bearer from lightning and illness. Sleeping beneath an oak was once thought to cure paralysis. If you catch an oak leaf before it lands on the ground in the fall, you will be free from colds all winter.

Medicinal: Boiling white oak acorns in a good-quality oil yields a substance that is excellent for aching joints. It can be applied as is or made into a cream. Decoctions made from oak leaves have a mild astringent quality that helps with swollen glands. Additionally, coffee made from roasted acorns aids digestion.

Culinary, Crafts: Early people honored the oak for its abundant edible fruit as much as they did for the durable nature of the tree. Some varieties bear better nuts than others, including the live oak, swamp white oak, and California white oak. Acorns can be roasted as a snack, or the meal may be used as bread grain and soup thickener. Oils obtained from acorns can be used in cooking and have a similar texture and quality to almonds.

A fun diversion for children is creating a rune set using acorn caps that can be painted with the symbols. Alternatively, the caps may be painted and strung together for various holiday decorations. Choose colors according to the season and use them on the Yule tree!

Gardening, Habitat: Most oaks prefer a slightly dry soil, with some rocks for good drainage. Harvest the leaves in spring for tinctures and decoctions. Acorns for coffee are best picked late in fall, then stored until spring.

Other: The chestnut oak is favored for tanning, while oak galls (a type of growth found on the leaves and twigs) are a component in ink. Truffles that grow as a by-product of oak trees are considered a delicacy in France. At the turn of the twentieth century, rural Americans used a mixture of oak sawdust, vinegar, and water to clean their bottles.

Oat
Avena sativa

Folk Names: Groats

History: In early days, oat straw stuffed mattresses. Culpeper mentions oats for external use against itching, and Gerald recommends it for fair skin.

Folklore, Superstition, Magic: Legends in Europe talk of a field spirit called the Oats Goat. The spirit is embodied in a doll made from the last sheaf collected from the field. This poppet symbolized continued fertility for the farmer and their family. Germany has similar customs, except the creature is a stallion instead of a goat. Carry an oat sprig to improve finances or keep one in your home, so everyone therein will never hunger.

Medicinal: Research suggests that athletes who eat a diet high in oats can reduce their cholesterol and improve their stamina. Oatmeal porridge with a bit of honey is an excellent fortifying food for those healing from illness or injury. Roasted oats may be brewed into coffee and taken as a laxative or to soothe hemorrhoids. Take two to three teaspoons daily for three days.

Culinary, Crafts: While oats are frequently in cereal as a source of vitamin B and calcium, my favorite use for them is in cookies. Here is one recipe:

- ¾ cup vegetable shortening
- 1 cup brown sugar, firmly packed
- ½ cup granulated sugar
- 1 egg
- ¼ cup milk
- 3 cups oats
- 1 tsp vanilla
- 1 cup flour
- ½ tsp baking soda
- ½ cup chopped nuts
- ½ cup raisins
- 1 cup butterscotch morsels
- Pinch of ginger (optional)

Preheat oven to 350 degrees Fahrenheit. Beat the shortening, sugars, egg, milk, and spices together until smooth. Add the flour, oats, and baking soda. Mix well. Fold in the remaining ingredients by hand and drop onto a greased cookie sheet with a teaspoon. Bake twelve to fifteen minutes or until golden brown. Yields four to five cookies.

Gardening, Habitat: Oats are native to Northern Europe, but grow well in most temperate regions. They require a fair amount of space for effective cultivation and should be harvested in early fall.

Other: Oatmeal facials and baths are excellent for the skin. If you or your children get chicken pox, make oatmeal soap to calm the itching.

Olive
Olea europaea

Folk Names: Minerva's tree (Rome)

History: The olive tree was first cultivated around 3500 BCE in Crete. Many ancient civilizations revered both the olive tree and its by-products. In Greece, the olive symbolized sagacity. In antiquity, it was common to carry or present an olive branch as a symbol of peace and goodwill. This tradition was so widespread that the olive remains a part of the United Nations flag.

Folklore, Superstition, Magic: The olive tree is perhaps best known in the biblical story of Noah and the Ark. In Greek mythology, Athens was named after Athena because she gifted the first olive trees to the city. Unsurprisingly, the tree is sacred to Athens. Many religious traditions use olive oil as a base for ritual anointing oils, which are also believed to have healing qualities. Olive branches left in a room promote peace between people. Adorning one's head with olive leaves improve fertility, while hanging them in the home offers protection against lightning and attracts good fortune. Romans felt olive oil worn on one's skin promoted joy.

Medicinal: Olive oil mixed with soup or other foods stimulates bowel movements. For external use, mix olive oil with egg whites and apply to soothe burns and bug bites.

Culinary, Crafts: Perhaps one of the most popular oils for cooking, olive oil brings out the flavor in herbs and foods.

Keep several savory mixtures in your home for different types of cooking (see Chapter Two for ideas).

Gardening, Habitat: Olive trees require a temperate climate to grow well. The leaves may be harvested anytime, while the fruit is harvested in late summer.

Other: Dab olive oil on patches of dry skin as needed.

―――――

Onion
Allium cepa

Folk Names: Onyoun

History: The onion likely originated in Egypt, where, like garlic, it was applied for many medicinal purposes. Alexander the Great's troops ate onions before battle for strength and courage. Centuries later, a physician in the 1100s recommended onion juice as a contraceptive.

Folklore, Superstition, Magic: Europeans used onions as a protective amulet against the plague. The Egyptians regarded the onion as an aphrodisiac and often prepared it for young couples on their wedding night. Eating onions regularly increases longevity, fosters hair growth, engenders passion, and fights obesity. To divine your future spouse, carve the names of four suitors into four onions and then plant them. According to British tradition, the first to sprout is your true love. Carry onions in your left pocket to protect yourself from disease or rub the juice on your scalp to help prevent balding. Dreaming of onions foretells good luck.

Medicinal: The Native Americans used wild onion juice to treat colds and insect bites. They applied poultices of baked onion to draw out infections, treat migraines, and soothe sunburns.

An onion's benefits are most substantial in raw form. Eating an onion or drinking the juice regularly may combat anemia, joint disorders, high blood sugar, and worms. Onion juice works similarly to clove oil for toothaches. A cooked onion alleviates congestion and—with a little butter—eases the pain of a sore throat.

Culinary, Crafts: Try stuffing onions as you might a green pepper. Remove one end of the onion and cut out all but several outer layers. Chop a third of the removed portion, sauté with garlic to taste, and mix with a favorite meat or other vegetables.

Anoint the exterior of the onion shell with olive oil, then fill it with your mixture. Bake at 300 degrees Fahrenheit in the oven until golden brown. If you wish, melt a little cheese over the top or drizzle with fresh butter.

Besides culinary applications, onion skins make a serviceable yellow, orange, or brown dye.

Gardening, Habitat: Onions grow well in a variety of conditions, but fare best in the northern hemisphere. Companion-plant them with cabbage and lettuce. Harvest in late summer or early fall when they fully mature.

Other: Mix an onion poultice with a little vinegar and apply regularly to bleach freckles. Use onion juice to clean your knives and brass to improve the shine in old leather.

———

Orange
Citrus aurantium

Folk Names: Golden apple of Hesperides, love fruit

History: Orange trees originated in central Asia. After the Crusades, they were brought to the Mediterranean and Europe, where they became popular as decorative trees for royal households. In marriage rituals, the orange represented both virginity and devotion, being a symbol of fruitfulness.

Folklore, Superstition, Magic: In Greek mythology, Zeus presented Hera with an orange at their wedding. Oranges and their dried peels often appear in spells for love and devotion between people. In China, oranges are believed to draw good fortune and prosperity.

Medicinal: Orange flower water is thought to improve sleep. Oranges offer a good quantity of vitamin C to combat colds and improve overall well-being.

Culinary, Crafts: Oranges are a favorite fruit for eating and juicing, and they also offer cooks a multitude of applications. I personally enjoy adding crushed oranges to honey as a barbecue baste or cooking them with beef and ginger for a sweet-tangy flavor. Oranges are also one of the best fruits to use in pomander (see Chapter Two).

Like many edible blossoms, orange flowers may be added to biscuits, jellies, butter, and beverages. Orange flower water is a good alternative to rose water in many recipes, and most stores carry both pre-prepared.

Gardening, Habitat: Oranges thrive in warm environments with no risk of frost.

Other: Orange blossom water was once favored for finger bowls and in a lady's bedchamber for refreshing the skin. The scent of orange calms anxiety. In the language of flowers, it represents chastity.

Orchid
Orchis spp.

Folk Names: Ancestor of fragrances, lizard orchid, satyrion, dog's stones, soldier's cullions, foolstones, foxstones

History: Orchids are fabled as the food of satyrs, and in China, people believed that true friendship bears the scent of orchids. They were most popular in Italy and Turkey for medicinal and culinary uses but found their way into English pantries as well. Parkinson believed distilled orchid petals made an effective aphrodisiac, while Dioscorides wrote of the bulb as improving virility.

Folklore, Superstition, Magic: Folklore says that orchids originated with Orchis, whose body parts became the first orchid flowers after a fight during a feast. A Turkish beverage called *salep* included orchid roots and was concocted specifically for passion. Carry the root of an orchid with you to attract a lover. Some say giving orchid root to another engenders desire.
Medicinal: The roots serve as a nerve tonic when boiled in water, then mixed with a little wine, lemon juice, and grated orange rind. Parkinson recommended the flowers for overall health and well-being, while Dioscorides said the root increased fertility.
Culinary, Crafts: Orchids are high in nutrients. Add the petals into sandwiches or make a soup with petals, rice, white wine, thin lemon slices, and water. This soup is also thought to be an aphrodisiac.
Gardening, Habitat: Most orchids are native to tropical and subtropical regions, but several species fare well in temperate climates. Most require good soil, drainage, regular watering, and indirect light, but this varies depending on the species.
Other: Keep the scent of orchids away from your clothes as moths love them! In the language of flowers, they represent the perfected man.

Pansy
Viola tricolor

Folk Names: Heartease, herb trinity, garden gate, idle love, banewort, garden violet, jump-ups, herb constancy, call-me-to-you, little-my-fancy, loving thoughts, stepfathers and stepmothers, three-faces, kiss-me-quick, St. Valentine's flower
History: There are over two hundred species of pansy whose name comes from the French *pensée*. Shakespeare, in *A Midsummers Night Dream*, uses the pansy as a love philter.

Folklore, Superstition, Magic: According to a Germanic legend, cows prayed to the gods to remove the fragrance of pansies so they could eat it without humans desiring it. Carrying the pansy will draw love. If you pick one early in the morning and there is still dew on its petals, it will rain.

Medicinal: In compresses or decoctions, the pansy is effective in treating minor skin irritations. Decoctions have a diuretic effect and seem to help rheumatoid arthritis when taken daily. Take three to four teaspoons between meals.

Culinary, Crafts: Among the Victorians, this was a favorite flower for pressing. Its blossoms are edible and can be made into wines, gelatin salads, and candies. To make a pansy syrup, cover some petals in water and steep over low flame until they turn translucent. Add an equal amount of sugar to the liquid and bring the mixture to a low boil. Place in an airtight bottle and refrigerate for use on pancakes, ice cream, and waffles.

Gardening, Habitat: Pansies prefer sandy, loamy soil on hillsides. Do not overexpose them to direct sunlight. Harvest the flowers and roots when the plant first comes into bloom.

Other: In the language of flowers, this unassuming blossom represents loving thoughts.

Parsley
Petroselinum crispum

Folk Names: Common parsley, Devil's oatmeal, percely

History: Romans thought that parsley caused impotence, and the people in the Middle Ages used it for death magic. Unsurprisingly, cow parsley has a myriad of negative folk names, including bad man's oatmeal and Devil's meat.

Conversely, the Greeks held parsley in high regard and used it for head wreaths to maintain good cheer. Brides in this region often wore headpieces filled with parsley. About one hundred years ago, it wasn't uncommon for a parent to tell a young one that babies come from parsley patches.

Folklore, Superstition, Magic: In Greek mythology, parsley originated from the blood of Archemorus after he was eaten by serpents. Thus, the Greeks used parsley as part of their funerary rites. In the Middle Ages, people served parsley with meals to prevent drunkenness.

If you need a little extra luck, sow parsley seeds in your garden on Good Friday.

One note of caution: if you are in love, never cut parsley fresh from your garden—this will cut off good feelings!

Medicinal: Early remedials recommended parsley in treating both swollen eyes and epilepsy. Today, parsley tea aids sleeplessness and coughing. It is rich in vitamins A, B, and C, and offers a good portion of calcium and iron. Sometimes, parsley greens or tea proves effective in treating rheumatism and boils, and it is periodically recommended for minor bladder problems. However, parsley may be detrimental if you are pregnant as it promotes menstruation.

Culinary, Crafts: The French love cooking with parsley, especially as a final touch to ham and grilled meats. In Northern Europe, people sometimes use deep-fried parsley as part of fondue. It is also nice when added fresh to salads, salad dressing, and sauces.

Gardening, Habitat: A native of Europe and the Mediterranean, parsley is easily cultivated in the garden. Soak the seeds overnight before sowing about half an inch down into the soil. Harvest the leaves throughout the growing season as desired and gather the seeds when they ripen.

Other: Chew a sprig of parsley to clear bad breath. Wash your face with parsley water to help clear your complexion. In the language of flowers, parsley represents entertainment and feasting, which is perhaps why it appears so frequently on restaurant plates today.

Pine
Pinus spp.

Folk Names: Scots pine, forest pine, sea pine, pinaster
History: The pine tree has well over eighty varieties. Its name derives from the Latin word *pinus,* meaning "fat." This may be due to the appearance of the rosins, tar, oils, and pitch produced by this tree.

In antiquity, the pine was revered because it stayed green all winter. It was believed that a powerful spirit dwelled in the tree and could be appeased with small gifts, particularly during colder months. Thus came the Yule tree with all its beauty.

The Egyptians used pine to make turpentine resin. The Saudi Arabians prescribed it for lung problems, and Hippocrates writes of pine as a remedy for severe colds.
Folklore, Superstition, Magic: In Greek mythology, the pine tree was created when Pitys, a nymph who loved Pan, scorned the attentions of the wind god, Boreas. Boreas struck Pitys to death on a rock in anger, and Pan caused the first pine to grow from her remains in his grief. Carry pinecones for long life and fertility. Burn the incense in your home to banish evil, decrease bad feelings, and attract money. Pine branches placed around the home avert illness, and, in Japan, people believe pine brings happiness to all who dwell within.
Medicinal: In the 1500s, pinecones were used to treat toothaches. Today, pine oil is regularly used as a disinfectant and mixed with water as a cleanser. The needles may be added to hot water as an inhalant for colds or to bathwater to increase circulation.
Culinary, Crafts: In Alaska, the inner bark of the scrub pine is pounded into a hard-tack traveler's bread. Pine nuts have come into fashion as a healthy snack food in recent years. These are commonly gathered from the sugar, nut, Torrey's, digger,

and big-cone pines. Of these, the big-cone pines yield nuts that are high in oils and sugar.

Gardening, Habitat: Pines thrive in well-drained, sandy soil, but each specimen has slightly different needs. Pick pine buds early in spring before they open completely. Harvest pine needles at any time unless they have already turned brown. Brown needles are only good for starting fires.

Other: Scatter pine needles under your pet's bed or stuff their pillow with pine to deter fleas and keep the house smelling fresh. In Japan's floral calendar, the pine is featured as January's flower and represents life. In the language of flowers, pine represents pity.

Pineapple
Ananas comosus

History: Between 1500 and 1700 CE, the pineapple was featured on confectioners' signboards. In Victorian America, it became an emblem of hospitality, featured often as a motif on furniture.

Folklore, Superstition, Magic: The scent of pineapple purportedly draws both luck and money. Burn pineapple in your home for either or carry a piece to improve your fortune.

Medicinal: Ripe pineapple is a good digestive aid, soothing gas and constipation. The juice has diuretic qualities, and the leaves ease painful menstruation when made into a tincture.

Culinary, Crafts: Pineapple is high in vitamins A and C. Use it as juice during the summer, in marinades for pork and chicken, and baking. To make pineapple fritters, start by making a batter using one cup of flour, a quarter teaspoon of salt, a third cup of milk, a half tablespoon of melted butter, one beaten egg white, and a dash of ginger and cinnamon. Mix them all together to form a thick batter. Next, add half a pound of diced pineapple to the batter and mix well before deep-frying. Sprinkle with powdered sugar or cinnamon sugar before serving.

Gardening, Habitat: Pineapples are native to tropical regions, specifically South America. They need soil that drains well and maintains moisture with moderate fertilizer.

Other: In the language of flowers, pineapple represents personal perfection.

Pomegranate
Punica granatum

Folk Names: Apple of Carthage

History: The Egyptian pharaoh Tuthmose brought the pomegranate from Asia into Egypt around 1500 BCE. Dioscorides wrote of its ability to expel worms. Some people believe the forbidden fruit of Genesis was not an apple but a pomegranate. Spain's national emblem is the pomegranate.

Folklore, Superstition, Magic: Because of its numerous seeds, the pomegranate is associated with fertility in Greece, China, Iran, and Rome. In China, people would present this fruit on altars as an offering when seeking to conceive a child. In America, it is traditional to make a wish before eating this fruit. Italians sometimes use pomegranate shoots for dowsing, and Iranians use it as an anti-witchcraft charm.

Medicinal: Pomegranate rind and bark are considered effective against tapeworms in decoction form; however, some countries restrict the use of bark due to its toxicity. Pomegranate juice can settle an upset stomach.

Culinary, Crafts: Pomegranate makes lovely wine and a tasty snack. The seeds are also sometimes used to flavor meats.

Gardening, Habitat: Native to Asia, pomegranates are widely cultivated. They are harvested in fall when the fruit ripens. The seeds are best started in December indoors, then transplanted to a sunny location. As the plant comes to blossom, snip the flowers regularly to increase fruit yield.

Other: The pomegranate represents hope in some Christian traditions, while in others, it symbolizes wealth.

Poplar
Populus spp.

Folk Names: Eadha (Ireland)
History: Poplar derives its scientific name from Latin, *arbor populi,* or "tree of the people," since it adorned public places. The best-known specimen is the famous balm of Gilead, *Populus balsamifera,* which is said to have marvelous restorative properties against burns. The Irish tree alphabet presents poplar as an emblem of old age and the season of fall. In this region, warriors' shields and measuring staves for grave sites and coffins were fashioned out of poplar wood.
Folklore, Superstition, Magic: The *Odyssey* mentions a poplar tree growing outside Calypso's cave. Legend says that Hercules wore a crown of poplar after slaying a giant. According to Euripides, the first poplar sprang from the tears of Phaethon's sisters.

Early people referred to the white poplar as the "tree of time" because the underside of its leaves is white like day, and the top is dark like night. This tree was often used to make water-witching wands. The black poplar was regarded as a sign of hopelessness in ancient Rome. If you wish to communicate better, place a piece of poplar under your tongue. To prevent robbery, plant one near your home.
Medicinal: In Europe, the bark was used in tincture form to treat fevers. Some Native American tribes applied aspen (a member of the poplar family) to flu, cold, and allergy symptoms. Today, poplar flowers are effective in skin creams that treat swelling or as an aspirin-like tincture.
Culinary, Crafts: Poplars are very flexible and make lovely ornamental decorations. The sap from some of these species makes excellent waterproof wood glue.

Gardening, Habitat: Poplars are hardy trees requiring nothing more than shallow, moist soil to grow.

Other: During the Middle Ages, poplar leaves symbolized the tenth hour of the day. The buds were frequently bruised and combed through the hair like a conditioner. Today, poplar is mainly used as paper pulp. The leaves and twigs make useful gold and brown dyes.

Pumpkin
Cucurbita pepo

Folk Names: Emperor of the garden (China)

History: Mayans used pumpkin to treat burns, while Europeans and the Puritans used the seeds mingled with honey and milk to cure worms.

Folklore, Superstition, Magic: Pumpkins are nearly synonymous with fall and All Hallows' Eve in the northern hemisphere. In the United States, pumpkins replaced turnips for jack-o'-lanterns, whose visage scared away any malevolent spirits wandering about on Halloween.

Medicinal: Decocted pumpkin pulp relieves intestinal irritation. The fruit also works well as a poultice for burns.

Culinary, Crafts: Pumpkin can be cooked like a vegetable similar to squash or used like a fruit for pies, breads, and cookies. It has a naturally high amount of water, resulting in moist baked goods. Some people combat intestinal worms with pumpkin seeds, and, though it isn't a cure, this practice seems to hold its weight in scientific studies.

Pumpkin seeds make a good snack food. Try them roasted with Worcestershire sauce, garlic powder, and butter.

Gardening, Habitat: Most likely native to North America and India, the pumpkin grows in a variety of climates and soils, preferring warmer temperatures. It is harvested in fall when the fruit matures.

Other: Mash the seeds with almond oil and apply to the skin to keep it soft and smooth.

In China, this vegetable represents health and abundance.

Quince
Cydonia oblonga

Folk Names: Flowering quince
History: During the time of Hippocrates, people used quince as an astringent.

Dioscorides recommended the oil to treat infected wounds, while Pliny mentions that it protects against the evil eye.

Folklore, Superstition, Magic: In ancient Rome, the altars to Venus were often adorned with this fruit because it was believed to engender love. Romans exchanged quince as part of marriage rituals to seal the vow, assure fidelity, and encourage joy. Quince seeds are considered protective talismans when carried.

Medicinal: The unripe fruit is effective against diarrhea, while quince juice is a serviceable mouthwash for sore gums and canker sores. Quince acts as a digestive aid when cooked and consumed.

Culinary, Crafts: One of the best uses for quince is as a jelly. Begin with three pounds of cored ripe fruit. Put this in a large pot, cover with water, and cook over a low flame for one hour. Strain the resulting juice through cheesecloth, then measure a quarter cup of sugar for every cup of juice. Mix on the stove, stirring regularly until the sugar dissolves, and the mixture reaches 220 degrees Fahrenheit. Skim again and place in sterilized jars topped with paraffin. If desired, stir in raisins and chopped nuts before canning.

Gardening, Habitat: This native of Central Asia prefers deep, heavy, damp soil and ripens in fall. The flowering variety, *Chaenomeles lagenaria,* makes a beautiful addition to lawns and gardens.

Other: The word "marmalade" comes from the Portuguese word *marmelo,* which is another name for quince.

Radish
Raphanus sativus

Folk Names: Rapuns, garden radish

History: As early as 400 BCE, Egyptians used radish like currency when paying the pyramid builders. Romans used radish oil to treat skin ailments, and in 600 CE, the Chinese recommended it to aid digestion.

Folklore, Superstition, Magic: Carry a radish as a talisman against the evil eye or to improve passion. Eat one before breakfast to overcome all difficulties of the day.

Medicinal: Radishes eaten before meals improve sluggish appetites. Sliced radishes, sprinkled with sugar, macerated for a full day, and then pressed through a cloth, can be taken in tablespoonfuls to alleviate coughs.

Culinary, Crafts: Radish is most seen in salads and vegetable platters.

Gardening, Habitat: Native to South Asia, radishes grow well in temperate climates and can easily be cultivated in window boxes. Plant several small crops throughout the growing season and harvest them as soon as they grow large enough.

Other: At the Japanese Festival of Seven Herbs (January 7), people make a ritual rice broth with radishes during the Hour of the Hare (6:00 a.m.).

Raspberry
Rubus idaeus

Folk Names: Wild raspberry, thimbleberry, blackcap raspberry
History: During their travels, warriors of the Crusades often found raspberries, which provided them much pleasure during difficult days. Some Native American tribes had a special ritual that honored this berry. In the 1700s, raspberry flowers and fruit mixed with honey were used to treat puffy eyes and boils.
Folklore, Superstition, Magic: Some people carry raspberry leaves as a love charm. Due to their abundance, raspberries can represent prosperity and abundant joy. Plant a bush to improve finances or overall happiness.
Medicinal: Raspberry leaf tea is often recommended for menstrual cramps and proves an excellent tonic during the later stages of pregnancy. The bark and root made into a tincture create a mild astringent that combats nausea and vomiting. Gargle with raspberry vinegar to ease a sore throat. In the early 1900s, raspberry vinegar with cloves and honey was recommended for asthma.
Culinary, Crafts: Soak four cups of fresh raspberries in two tablespoons of rum and a hint of honey or sugar to taste. Serve chilled with whipped cream and slivered almonds. For a unique summer barbecue, marinate chicken in raspberry juice or vinegar in the refrigerator before grilling with raspberry honey.
Gardening, Habitat: Raspberry is native to Europe and Asia, growing well in most temperate regions. For best results, use well-drained, humus-laden soil that isn't overly packed.

Harvest the leaves in late spring or early summer and the berries when ripened.

Other: In the language of flowers, raspberries represent remorse. People from the Phillipines use raspberry vines to indicate grief and to protect the home from a wandering deceased spirit.

───────

Rose
Rosa spp.

Folk Names: Flower of love, queen of the flowers, China rose

History: The rose has been the reigning matriarch of blossoms for more than three thousand years. It is renowned for both its beauty and versatility. Roses originated in Persia, where they were recognized for their nutritional value. The fabled Hanging Gardens of Babylon contained over three hundred varieties of roses.

The Romans considered it a prized aromatic and food item, while Arab leaders used rose water to wash their clothes as a sign of respect for their position. Statues of Cupid were often crowned with roses since they both represented love. In 812 CE, Charlemagne prioritized cultivating roses for his garden. In 1049 CE, it became customary for the pope to bestow a golden rose as a token of honor.

In the language of flowers, roses represent silence, and during the Middle Ages, any conversation that took place beneath one was considered confidential. This is where the term *sub rosa* originates.

Folklore, Superstition, Magic: Having been born of Aphrodite's blood, this flower has always had strong associations with love magic. Numerous love potion recipes include rose petals. As a tea, roses bring prophetic dreams, and, if sprinkled around your home, they bring peace. Hold a rose petal in one hand while thinking of a question, then snap your hand shut quickly. If the petal makes a loud snapping sound, the answer is yes.

Medicinal: Rose hips have more vitamin C than oranges and make an excellent tea for colds and flu. As an aromatic, the smell of roses decreases anxiety and depression. When you have a headache, dab rose water on your temples for relief.

To make an excellent sore throat remedy, steep two cups of rose petals, half an orange with rind, half a teaspoon of rosemary, and one slice of lemon in one cup of honey. Strain and store in an airtight container. Take one tablespoon at a time. This is also good as a sauce for poultry.

Culinary, Crafts: Rose oil is a favorite scent for potpourri, candles, and linen. In the kitchen, the rose can add beauty and flavor to almost anything. Petals may be made into jams, syrups, sandwiches, soups, wines, and waters. Rose water is known within the Arabic world as the *dew of paradise.*

To make rose water, steep rose petals in warm water until they lose all color. Strain the water and repeat with fresh petals until you're happy with the aroma, then refrigerate until use. This is especially nice for finger bowls and as a mild flavoring in baking. Rose water also makes a wonderful aromatic for wine.

To make rose parfait, layer your serving bowls with fresh petals and place chopped dates, rose petal jam, and two tablespoons of orange juice. Let this soak for three to four hours in the refrigerator, then serve with a drizzle of almond or orange-flavored cream.

Gardening, Habitat: To keep your roses free of ants and some other insects, plant garlic around them. According to

British folklore, stealing a cutting or seed to start a rosebush is necessary if you want it to bloom abundantly.

Roses like clay-laden soils. Prune the bush regularly in spring and pick the flowers as they appear for more abundant blossoms. **Other:** Rose oil is an acclaimed skin beautifier. In the language of flowers, the yellow rose represents friendship; the white, peace or death; and the red, passion and love.

Rosemary
Rosmarinus officinalis

Folk Names: Sea dew, polar plant, old man, romero
History: Ancient Greek students used sprigs of rosemary when preparing for school exams, and, in Roman times, rosemary served as a symbol of fidelity between lovers. In the Middle Ages, it was placed under pillows to keep nightmares away. It was also used in metheglin, a type of honey and herb wine. During this period and long after, rosemary was an important medicinal herb used for joint problems. Nowadays, rosemary extract is used as a food preservative in place of chemical formulas, and long-distance runners rub it on their muscles to prevent strain.
Folklore, Superstition, Magic: In the Middle Ages, cunning folk mixed rosemary with the hair of a mad dog to cure its bite. This is how the phrase "hair of the dog that bit you" originated. This herb was also believed to bring joy to the living and peace to the dead. Around the mid-1700s, rosemary bushes became the emblem for peddlers who sold donkey's milk. If rosemary was able to grow in a garden abundantly, it was believed that the household was run by a woman.

Carrying rosemary protects the bearer against witchcraft and brings luck. A morning meal of rosemary flowers preserved in sugar, then sprinkled with salt, improves vision.
Medicinal: A medieval writer claimed that candying and eating rosemary flowers brings joy and comfort. An ointment made

from rosemary eases sore joints and muscles. Fresh rosemary is also a good ingredient to mix with other herbs for liniment. There is some evidence that suggests burning dried rosemary may help eliminate airborne germs. Rosemary oil stimulates circulation, and a tincture of rosemary helps combat depression.

Culinary, Crafts: Rosemary is a very sweet herb and can be used in place of mint. Whole, fresh sprigs can be frozen, making this a very serviceable herb. It is good for cooking and garnishing many dishes. Throw a small bundle on the grill before barbecuing meats, especially duck or game.

Rosemary adds a zesty flavor to white wine or honey. To add it to wine, simply steep a handful of fresh stalks in a bottle of wine, keep it closed for two to three days, then strain and chill. To add it to honey, warm a handful of rosemary flowers with eight ounces of honey over a low flame. Strain when the herb looks almost translucent, then store for use.

Gardening, Habitat: A native of Greece, Italy, Spain, and North Africa, rosemary grows well in temperate regions with warm, semidry climates and well-drained soil. Harvest the herb in midsummer after flowering.

Other: Rosemary tincture used as a hair rinse eases dandruff. Rosemary is also a potent aromatic that can be used in homemade incense and as part of sachets to deter moth infestation. Rosemary's scent improves energy, allays headache, and is an excellent additive for smelling salts. Rosemary is a popular herb for bridal bouquets because of its ability to strengthen love. In the language of flowers, rosemary represents remembrance.

Rowan
Sorbus acuparia

Folk Names: Mountain ash, quicken, wicken tree, witchwood, sorb apple

History: Rowan gets its name from the Norse *runa,* meaning "to charm." Graves indicate that rowan may have been used by druids for divination, which may explain its presence near many stone circles.

Folklore, Superstition, Magic: Place a rowan outside your home to protect it from evil and lightning strikes. The Irish used rowan stakes in the body of a person whose ghost was thought to be haunting a home or region. Conversely, the Irish sometimes lit rowan fires to call on spirits for aid! Carrying rowan berries protects your health and well-being. Rowan twigs bound with red thread are an ancient anti-witchcraft charm.

Medicinal: Drink a berry infusion to fight diarrhea and hemorrhoids or gargle it to ease a sore throat.

Culinary, Crafts: The fruit of the mountain ash makes a serviceable jelly with a high amount of vitamin C, but all seeds must be removed from the fruit before cooking as the seeds are toxic.

Gardening, Habitat: A native to the northern hemisphere, this tree is not particular about its soil and can endure dry conditions well.

Other: Rowan is a popular alternative to yew in bows for archery in Wales.

Saffron
Crocus sativus

Folk Names: *Karcom* (Hebrew)
History: Because of its cost, saffron has been considered the herb of kings and was often used to dye royal robes. It appeared on altars across the world as an offering to divine figures, including Ra in Egypt and Brahma in Hindu regions. King Solomon's garden had a plot of saffron, and it is called *karcom* in the Song of Solomon (4:14). As a point of interest, saffron is expensive because it takes about 35,000 flowers to make one ounce of spice.

Folklore, Superstition, Magic: The Phoenicians made ritual cakes with saffron to honor Ashtoreth. Some Persian people wore saffron near their navel during pregnancy to ensure quick births, and they also used sprigs of saffron to raise the winds. Wearing saffron in your hair prevents drunkenness, and the scent is said to make crocodiles weep. Among the people of India and Greece, it was considered a potent aphrodisiac, while Arabs kept a piece with them to allay depression.

Medicinal: In the medicine cabinet, saffron must be used carefully, as large quantities can be toxic. Some herbalists recommend it as an appetite aid, mild sexual stimulant, menstruation stimulant, and treatment for colds and insomnia. In aromatherapy, saffron is said to quicken spirits and bring merriment.

Culinary, Crafts: Saffron should be used in minute portions when cooking—a little bit goes a long way. For a unique treat, try this recipe:

- ¾ cup sugar
- ¼ pound sliced almonds
- ½ tsp saffron
- 4 pieces dark toast
- ¾ cup butter, melted
- 2 ¼ cups milk

Place the pieces of toast in a large saucepan and cover them with the melted butter. In a separate pot, boil the milk together with the sugar, almonds, and saffron. Mix well. Pour this into the pan containing the toast and continue boiling until it thickens. Chill and serve with a drizzle of sweet cream for dessert. Serves two.

Gardening, Habitat: A native to India, saffron does well in the Middle East, Italy, and France. It is harvested in early fall.

Other: Some people swear that adding a sprig of saffron to your canary's water increases the bird's singing. In the language of flowers, it represents mirth or marriage. While the Greeks and Romans used saffron to dye royal robes, the Irish used it for coloring bed linen.

Sage
Salvia officinalis

Folk Names: Sawge, garden sage, healer of all ills (medieval)

History: Sage takes its name from the Latin word *salvare,* meaning "to save." Among Greeks, people ate sage to improve the mind. It was a sacred herb among Romans, who first offered the plant wine and then harvested it without any iron tools. They believed that sage protected pregnant people, improved fertility, and extended life. Sage's popularity continued well into the Middle Ages, appearing in nearly every medicinal preparation. Sage tea was also very popular in China and Europe during the 1700s.

Folklore, Superstition, Magic: Sage was favored by Zeus. If you are wise, it will grow abundantly near your home, but if the head of the house is sick, it will wilt. The people of the Renaissance combined sage and honey to heal throat infections, a combination still used today. Some ancient Egyptian people believed that drinking sage juice before lying with their spouse would ensure immediate conception.

Carry sage with you to encourage prudence, protect against wandering spirits, and turn away the evil eye. Drink a tea from sage as people of old once did, believing it will improve hair growth and enhance color.

Medicinal: Purple sage is used for most medicinal products, except for gargles, which use wood sage. The best time to harvest and dry sage for medicinal use is spring.

For chapped lips, boil four tablespoons of sage in a half cup of water for about forty-five minutes or until the juice cooks down into a syrup. Apply as needed.

Sage also helps with digestion. Add two or three fresh leaves to your coffee or a cup of hot water and leave them for about five minutes, then enjoy. This same tea chilled provides relief for diarrhea in children. It should not be used by pregnant people as it is a hormonal stimulant.

If you feel a cold coming, place sage leaves in a cup of warm milk and drink it before bed. Rub fresh leaves on insect bites for relief and drink an infusion thrice daily to allay a sore throat or irregular menstruation.

Culinary, Crafts: Garden sage is the most common variety in cooking. It has a slightly bitter, lemony flavor and is a regular ingredient for poultry seasoning and stuffing. Sage also tastes good with cheese or as a bread flavoring. In the Middle East, people eat sage shoots like salad. Try wrapping fresh fronds around Cornish hen before cooking. Medieval peoples used sage in many dishes, including conserves and creams. Sage was also popular in scenting wines, especially in Germany. Here is a sage wine recipe for you to try:

- o 1 gallon water
- o 6 lb raisins
- o 1 cup sage leaves

Bring the water to a full rolling boil, then cool down to lukewarm. Meanwhile, finely chop the raisins and place them in a large, non-aluminum container with the sage. Pour the water over them and let sit for one week, stirring daily. Press out all the liquid and put it into a glass gallon container with an airtight lid. Let this sit undisturbed in a cool area for another six months. Finally, siphon off the clear liquid into wine bottles, cork them tightly, and let the contents age for a year before drinking.

Gardening, Habitat: A native to Mediterranean regions, sage likes a sunny climate and dry soil. It does not need fertilizer to fare well. Sow the seeds in early spring, separating them eighteen inches apart after sprouting. Harvest any one of the over five hundred species in summer and protect the plants with mulch in winter.

Other: Sage rinse is good for dandruff: combine two teaspoons of herb, one cup of water, and one teaspoon of alcohol, shake, and apply.

Use finely powdered sage as a deodorant. Alternatively, add two teaspoons to a half cup of cornstarch for similar results. This can also be sprinkled in shoes. Mix finely powdered sage with baby powder or baking soda and use it as an antiperspirant. For an effective aftershave, mix sage water with rubbing alcohol. Sage is sometimes used as an herbal tobacco. When sage burns, it helps eliminate odors in the home and alleviates airborne germs. In the language of flowers, sage represents domestic virtue.

St. John's Wort
Hypericum perforatum

Folk Names: Devil's fight, goat weed, herb John, Tipton weed, *y fendigedig* (Welsh)

History: St. John's wort originated in Assyria and was brought to Europe by the Crusaders. The genus *Hypericum* has Greek origins, meaning "above the icon." This refers to the use of St. John's wort around various carvings to keep evil influences away from the city.

St. John's wort was favored in the ancient pharmacopeia and magical circles for its power. Medicinally, the plant was used for emotional or nervous disorders. Metaphysically, people believed it protected the bearer from malevolent entities.

Folklore, Superstition, Magic: Carrying this herb keeps colds at bay and attracts potential lovers. If the blossoms are gathered on Midsummer's Day, they will keep the bearer safe from insanity and from ghosts.

Never step on this plant or a fairy horse will rise from beneath your feet and carry you off.

Medicinal: Herbalists recommend St. John's tincture (half a teaspoon of herb and one cup of water, taken three times daily) for nervous conditions and tension. It seems to also ease the symptoms of menopause. Externally, St. John's oil can be rubbed into cramped areas and relieve the effects of itchy bug bites. Using too much of this herb may cause photosensitivity or dermatitis.

Culinary, Crafts: A yellow and red dye can be obtained from the tips using chrome and tin mordants, respectively.

Gardening, Habitat: St. John's wort grows wild in most of the world. It prefers plenty of sun and chalky soil. Harvest the tips when they flower in midsummer.

Other: Use St. John's wort in a dream pillow to inspire prophetic visions, especially of future loves.

———————

Savory
Satureja hortensis

Folk Names: Garden savory, summer savory, donkey pepper, bean herb, *bohnenkraut*

History: The Romans likely introduced this herb to Europe, but it was not readily cultivated until around the ninth century in Italy. Virgil grew savory to keep his bees happy.

The Tudors included savory to make mazes in herb gardens, and the British colonists packed savory when they came to North America.

Folklore, Superstition, Magic: In Greek mythology, the satyrs loved savory and used it as a passion-inducing herb. In the Middle Ages, it was mixed with rose oil to cure deafness.

Medicinal: Rub a fresh leaf from this plant on any insect bite, especially bee stings, for fast relief. Or make a poultice for more difficult skin irritations.

Culinary, Crafts: As an alternative to pepper or thyme, try adding savory to game stews or lentil soup.

Gardening, Habitat: A native to Europe and Mediterranean regions, savory grows well in any sunny, temperate area with well-aerated soil. Snip the tops off first to extend your harvesting season.

Other: Savory's aroma is good for improving one's spirits.

Strawberry
Fragaria vesca

Folk Names: Child of the soil (Virgil), food of the Golden Age (Ovid)

History: Legend claims that John the Baptist lived on a diet of strawberries. The strawberry leaf became the emblem of English nobility and was placed on coronets.

Folklore, Superstition, Magic: Strawberries are sacred to the Norse goddess Frigga and later became associated with the Virgin Mary. Carry strawberry leaves as a charm to attract good luck. Farmers in Bavaria tie a bundle of berries to their cows as a gift to elves in exchange for abundance.

Medicinal: Strawberry leaf tea is a healthy choice for fever or anemia. The fruit, especially wild berries, strengthen the liver and spleen, but in large quantities can cause hives.

Strawberry juice added to skin cream improves the complexion and, when mingled with baking soda, helps remove teeth stains.
Culinary, Crafts: My favorite summer treat is fresh whole berries covered with sour cream and rolled in brown sugar. This combination is fast, easy, and tastes a lot like cheesecake.
Gardening, Habitat: Strawberries grow under various conditions ranging from slopes to rocky ground and woodlands, but they prefer cool, moist regions. Do not plant your strawberries into newly dug sod, as this attracts grubs that can destroy them.

Sweet Flag
Acorus calamus

Folk Names: Myrtle flag, sweet grass, sweet cane, sweet root, sweet rush, sedge
History: Sweet flag has been recognized as a stomach tonic since ancient times when it was used in Ayurvedic and Egyptian medicine. A botanist introduced it to Europe in the sixteenth century. The herb is in the Bible under the name of the species *calamus*. As late as the 1800s, some churches used this herb for strewing on the floor during festival days.
Folklore, Superstition, Magic: In India and Egypt, people used sweet flag to inflame passion as early as 2,500 years ago. Carry strawberry leaves as a charm to attract good luck.
Medicinal: The roots of this plant have long been used in India, Europe, and the United States to calm stomach problems, improve appetites, and ease tension. For fever, a decoction is best; for maldigestion, a tincture; and for toothache, a root chew.

Culinary, Crafts: Sweet flag may substitute cinnamon, but disputes over its safety in higher concentrations suggest this is not a good idea. This herb is better used in making sweet bags.
Gardening, Habitat: Sweet flag probably originated in India, but grows well in any damp soil, especially near a water source. Use it as part of a water garden.
Other: None.

Tansy
Tanacetum vulgare

Folk Names: Bitter buttons, parsley fern
History: In Italy, the gift of a tansy declares animosity. In Greek mythology, tansy flowers gave Ganymede his immortality as the gods' cupbearer. Culpeper recommended that people place tansy near their navels to prevent miscarriage.
Folklore, Superstition, Magic: Place a sprig of tansy in your shoe come the winter months to protect from colds and fever.
Medicinal: Steep tansy for a fine digestive tea but do not consume it during pregnancy. The Chippewa Indians use tansy root soaked in water to ease sore throats, and in Newfoundland, people apply tansy poultices to sprains. A similar preparation with vinegar may be placed on bruises. Pregnant people take note: Tansy can stimulate menstruation.
Culinary, Crafts: Tansy can be added to pudding, cakes, fritters, and breads. Traditionally, this flower scents Easter puddings and Lenten cakes. They are more favored, however, as vibrant dried flowers for crafts because their petals keep their hue for a long time. The tansy top also makes a dark yellow dye.
Gardening, Habitat: Tansy is easily cultivated by seed or division and requires no special soil. It is native to Europe and flowers in late summer.
Other: Growing tansy near your home deters ants, wasps, and flies. In the language of flowers, tansy represents a declaration of war.

Tarragon
Artemisia dracunculus

Folk Names: None.

History: Tarragon is related to mugwort. It was first introduced to Europe by Moorish invaders who brought it from Siberia. Our modern name "tarragon" may come from the Arabic *tharkhoum.* The French term for the herb, *estragon,* translates roughly to "little dragon."

Folklore, Superstition, Magic: The Roman scholar Pliny claimed this herb hindered weariness. For this purpose, put a sprig in your shoe before a long journey. Ancient people thought it could cure snakebite because of the root's serpentine appearance. In France, people used it to treat mad dog bites.

Medicinal: While tarragon remained mostly a culinary herb throughout history, it did find its way in the herbalist's kit, as was traditional for pantry spices.

For poor digestion, intestinal problems, and colic, infuse one teaspoon of tarragon, one quarter of an inch of vanilla bean, and a little sugar in one cup of water. Drink after meals. This tea also promotes urination and allays sleeplessness. Do not use during pregnancy as it may cause miscarriage.

Culinary, Crafts: Use tarragon similarly to parsley, finely chopped on meats, vegetables, in vinegars, and in salads. Be stingy with its application, however, as tarragon, like dragons, can be overpowering.

For a wonderful poultry sauce, try this recipe:

- ⅓ cup wine vinegar
- 2 chives
- 2 tsp chopped, fresh garlic
- 2 tsp dried tarragon
- 5 egg yolks
- 1 cup butter
- Salt and pepper to taste

Mix the vinegar, chives, garlic, and tarragon in a saucepan. Simmer until liquid is reduced by half. Add the egg yolks and beat the entire mixture until thick. Turn down the heat a little, then stir in the butter. This yields about two and a half cups of sauce, which is enough for four healthy servings. Don't forget to dip your rolls!

Gardening, Habitat: Native to the Himalayas, tarragon may be cultivated in most gardens. Harvest the aerial parts in late summer. Start new plants every four years, or they will lose their aroma and flavor.

Other: Tarragon grows exceptionally well indoors, allowing you to enjoy its flavor year-round. Otherwise, preserve it for a year by freezing it or by placing freshly picked and cleaned leaves in your favorite vinegar and sealing it tightly. If mingled into an outdoor garden, tarragon enhances vegetable growth.

Thyme
Thymus vulgaris

Folk Names: Garden thyme, wild thyme, mother of thyme, brotherwort

History: Thyme is native to the Mediterranean region and was known to the ancient Egyptians and Etruscans as an embalming herb. It was introduced to Britain by the Romans. Greek legend has it that thyme sprouted from the tears of Helen of Troy. The Greeks often used fresh thyme on the altars to their gods and burned it to purify their temples. Culpeper espoused thyme as a lung treatment.

Folklore, Superstition, Magic: Thyme represents valor in the language of flowers, echoing the Greek word *thymus,* which means "bravery." This may be why Romans believed thyme endowed courage when consumed. Thyme and beer soup was once thought to overcome shyness.

During the Middle Ages, a sprig of thyme was a common emblem for a lady's favor and was supposed to provide its bearer with bravery in battle. Since thyme was sacred to the fairies, some Europeans believed eating it would allow one to sneak a glimpse of the wee folk. It was planted on grave sites to console unhappy ghosts or burned in incense to improve health. According to Parkinson, drinking thyme tea mixed with rose vinegar before bed keeps nightmares away. Alternatively, sleep on a thyme pillow to uplift your spirit. Rinse skin in thyme water to increase beauty or smell it to gain courage.

Medicinal: Thyme is a good all-purpose tonic that eases coughs. It is an effective antiseptic, mild stimulant for the respiratory system, digestive aid, and antispasmodic. Take an infusion three times daily with honey to combat colds and chew the leaves for sore throats.

The flowering tips of thyme are best used for herbal treatments. Make sure they are free of debris before use. Thyme may be prepared in gargles and on compresses for sores and minor joint pain. Rub the fresh leaves on your skin to relieve itchy bug bites.

Add a little to your bathwater to improve circulation and complexion or treat arthritis.

Culinary, Crafts: Persians liked their thyme fresh and often nibbled on the flowers from the garden. In dried, fresh, or cooked form, thyme complements the flavor of meat, poultry, fish, soups, stews, butter, vinegars, and an assortment of vegetables. Because thyme comes in many varieties, its taste can often replace other spices. For example, lemon thyme can replace lemon when cooking poultry, and nutmeg thyme tastes much like our favorite pie spice.

Gardening, Habitat: Thyme thrives around the world in temperate zones, preferring sunny, well-drained banks that are high in chalk. Harvest the aerial parts in mid to late summer. I grow creeping thyme at home, and it flourishes wonderfully in hanging window pots.

Other: Add thyme to your wash water to cleanse and refresh the skin. The aroma of thyme helps bring restful sleep and lifts depression.

Patricia Telesco ――――――○

Tomato
Solanum lycopersicum

Folk Names: Love apple
History: Tomatoes were often used in Asia as remedials. Upon their introduction to Europe in the sixteenth century, tomatoes were regarded as potentially poisonous due to their relationship to nightshade. Tomatoes were not widely used until the 1700s, primarily in sauce and in preparing *ket chop* (ketchup).
Folklore, Superstition, Magic: Carry tomato seeds to attract love or eat more tomatoes to improve your fortune.
Medicinal: Studies suggest that ten servings of cooked tomatoes weekly may reduce the risk of prostate cancer. They supply high amounts of vitamin C and potassium.
Culinary, Crafts: Unlike many vegetables, tomatoes are healthier cooked. As a side dish, add lightly fried tomatoes with basil and garlic to pilaf.
Gardening, Habitat: Oddly enough, since tomatoes are related to potatoes, the two can sometimes be successfully grafted together for a *pomatoe,* which grows potatoes below ground and tomatoes above!

In cooler environments, plant them indoors, then transplant them after the last frost. Adding potash to an average, light soil increases tomato yields. Do not overwater your plants, or they will grow too tall and thin, providing little support to the fruit. Nettle and asparagus are two good companion plants for tomatoes.
Other: None.

Turmeric
Curcuma longa

Folk Names: Jaundice plant
History: A native of India, turmeric is a well-known culinary spice that is also used in Ayurvedic medicine.

Folklore, Superstition, Magic: Hawaiians use turmeric as a magical herb for cleansing.

Medicinal: Research into turmeric's application in western medicine began in the 1970s. A turmeric tea strengthens the liver, decreases acidity, and eases the pain of arthritis. It also shows potential in decreasing cholesterol and reducing the chances of heart attack.

In tincture or paste form, apply it to eczema and other itchy skin conditions three times daily for relief. Turmeric powder mixed with calendula in powder or cream can fight athlete's foot.

Culinary, Crafts: The taste of turmeric is perfect for potatoes, eggs, and many rice dishes.

Gardening, Habitat: This member of the ginger family needs well-drained soil and high humidity. The rhizome is best harvested in winter and is used in both cooking and healing.

Other: None.

Valerian
Valeriana officinalis

Folk Names: All-heal (Middle Ages), vandal root, garden heliotrope, St. George's herb

History: Romans used valerian as a sedative, while Dioscorides named it *phu* because of its terrible smell. Legend claims that the Pied Piper used valerian to attract cats when trying to rid Hamelin of rats.

Valerian derives its name from the Latin *valere*, meaning "to be well," due to its calming effect.

Folklore, Superstition, Magic: Sorcerers used valerian as part of rituals to commune with spirits, while the Arabs believed valerian encouraged lust. Hung in a window or doorway, this herb protects a home from evil influences.

Medicinal: Valerian tea is an effective choice for stress-related disorders, especially insomnia, but should not be combined with any sleep-inducing medication. You may wish to mix this with mint, as valerian smells like old sweat socks.

Culinary, Crafts: Valerian makes an excellent addition to herb baths, but beyond this, it is a lovely plant to grow, coming in numerous colors to highlight floral and herb gardens.

Gardening, Habitat: Native to Europe, valerian is most fragrant when grown in dry regions but takes well to wet regions too. Thin it regularly and harvest two-year-old roots in the fall.

Other The scent of valerian deters moths but attracts cats. The root's oils are used commercially in flavoring beverages.

———

Vervain
Verbena officinalis

Folk Names: Herb of enchantment, holy herb, pigeon grass, verbena, herb of grace, enchanter's plant, sacred herb (Dioscorides), wild hyssop, simpler's joy, fever weed

History: Hippocrates wrote about vervain and Romans used it in rituals to honor Jupiter. The druids applied this herb for both magic and medicine. In Greece, people used vervain to wash the altars of Zeus before special feasts, while Persians used the herb in sun worship. Gerard believed this herb encouraged joy.

Folklore, Superstition, Magic: The Anglo-Saxons carried this herb as a charm against sorcery. In Persia, wizards regarded it as an herb that grants wishes, and both Romans and people of Tudor England ate vervain as an aphrodisiac. Vervain and dill bound together are an anti-witchcraft charm. Bathing with vervain juice encourages the gift of prophecy. Crusaders claimed that vervain sprang from the blood of Christ's hands and thus was sometimes used in holy water. Wear a crown of vervain when you need protection or luck.

Medicinal: Use vervain in tincture form to relax and calm the nerves. As an infusion, it acts as a digestive aid. Vervain can help stimulate milk production for nursing parents but should not be used during pregnancy because it stimulates the uterus. For your complexion, try bruised vervain leaves mixed with vinegar to clear the skin.

Culinary, Crafts: The Turks enjoy salt flavored with vervain, and many early wine-making texts recommend it mingled with other fruits and herbs for wine making.

Gardening, Habitat: Vervain is easily cultivated in temperate regions, often among weeds. It prefers a sunny, well-drained soil. Harvest the aerial parts in summer after flowering. The traditional way of harvesting vervain entails finding the plant when neither the Sun nor Moon are in the sky, harvesting it with iron (never touching the plant directly), and then offering honey to the Earth in thanks.

Other: Vervain represents enchantment in the language of flowers. Rub vervain powder on your teeth as an alternative to toothpaste.

Violet
Viola odorata

Folk Names: Heart's ease, Johnny jumper, sweet violet

History: The Greeks wore violets to keep anger at bay during confrontations. It was also the emblem for Athens. Romans used these flowers in wine and Napoleon gave them to Josephine on their anniversaries. An Arabic proverb likens them to the beauty of faith. Two thousand years ago, Italians planted violets with onions, believing this would improve the flower's scent. The violet remains a very popular flower, serving as the state symbol for Illinois, New Jersey, Rhode Island, and Wisconsin.

Folklore, Superstition, Magic: In Roman mythology, Venus once asked Cupid to compare her beauty to some maidens. When Cupid preferred the maidens, Venus beat them until they were sorely bruised. To compensate for this cruelty, Cupid turned them into violets.

Carry a violet flower in your pocket for luck and protection. Drinking violet water inspires love. If you sleep with violets in the room, it relieves a headache and ensures a restful night. In some magical traditions, violets act as charms against ghosts.

Medicinal: Violets are good in cold teas. In an infusion, they make an excellent facial steam, skin cleanser, and emollient. Use a violet leaf poultice to treat swelling and a decoction as a comforting foot bath.

Culinary, Crafts: Violets are just as versatile as roses. Make them into jam, ices, syrups, cakes, wines, soups, salads, and aromatic honey. Additionally, violet water makes a lovely finger bowl for formal dinners.

To make a violet souffle, begin by melting one tablespoon of butter in a saucepan. Add one tablespoon of flour and stir until combined. Then, add a half cup of hot milk and cook over a low flame until thickened. In a separate bowl, mix a capful of brandy with one to two tablespoons of sugar and one egg yolk. Beat the egg white until stiff, then stir into the brandy with a quarter cup of finely chopped candied violets. Blend this into the original milk mixture, then pour into a souffle dish, baking until lightly browned. Decorate with fresh flowers and a dollop of vanilla-flavored heavy cream.

As a craft item, violets are lovely in pressed flower arrangements, retaining their color well.

Gardening, Habitat: Sow violets in rich soil, where they will receive both sun and shade. Harvest the flowers in spring and the roots in fall.

Other: In the language of flowers, the yellow violet represents joy; the dame's violet, watchfulness; and the blue, devotion.

Walnut

Juglans spp.

Folk Names: Jupiter's acorns (Roman), butternut, oil nut

History: Walnuts have long been considered "brain food" because they resemble the human brain. They were brought into Italy from Persia through Greece in the early Christian era. Greeks and Romans served stewed nuts at weddings to represent fertility, and Culpeper recommended green walnut husks as a remedy for sore throats.

In the 1700s, a walnut tree became a predominant emblem for many cabinetmakers' business signs.

Folklore, Superstition, Magic: Some Europeans consider walnut a witch tree, yet placing a whole walnut under a chair will keep a witch from moving. Walnut branches gathered at Easter and kept in the home act as a protective charm against lightning until the next year.

An ancient charm used spiders encased in walnut shells to banish sickness or bind an enemy.

Medicinal: Research conducted in California indicated that one to two ounces of walnuts weekly reduce the risk of heart attacks. Walnuts have high quantities of vitamin E but are also high in fat, so take care. Use the oil in cooking to help decrease gas.

Culinary, Crafts: Besides their traditional role in baking, people in the Middle East use walnuts in rice and sauces and frequently mix them with dates and oranges.

Walnut oil is a base medium for various types of oil compounds (see Chapter Two).

Gardening, Habitat: Of the ten or so species, all walnuts are hardy trees that enjoy good, semidry soil. To prevent walnut caterpillar infestation, treat the trees before spring growth.

Other: Black walnut leaves keep away flies and ants.

Watermelon
Citrullus vulgaris

Folk Names: None

History: Watermelon existed in Egypt over four thousand years ago. It was used to combat diseases caused by demons and was sacred to the god Set. It came to America from Africa through the slave trade.

Folklore, Superstition, Magic: Some people believe watermelon aids in weight gain. In Egyptian mythology, Set's semen gave birth to this fruit.

Medicinal: Wall paintings dated to 2600 BCE in Egypt appear to show watermelons used as a remedy for constipation and nervousness. Mashed watermelon seeds expel worms. The fruit and juice of watermelon are considered a fair source of iron and combat the symptoms of heat exhaustion. Eating watermelon decreases gas and improves urine flow.

Culinary, Crafts: On a hot summer day, nothing beats a cold watermelon filled with your choice of liquor. Cut a small hole in the melon and pour in any amount of potable you prefer. For example, add a small bottle of fruit-flavored vodka or berry brandy to a goodly sized melon. Replace the piece you cut out of the melon, then chill. Carve the melon lengthwise, carefully removing the fruit, and use the empty shell as a serving platter. Add fresh berries and enjoy.

For a nonalcoholic option, chill the melon and pour in some raspberry ginger ale prior to serving.

Gardening, Habitat: Watermelon prefers warm, temperate or tropical regions with good soil rich in humus. Water it regularly in hot weather and give the soil a fertilizer infusion mid-season. General cultivation is similar to that for cucumbers. Do not harvest the fruit until it is fully ripened on the vine—this improves sweetness.

Other: None

Wild Yam
Dioscorea villosa

Folk Names: Colic root, rheumatism root

History: The root's attributes led to the creation of the first contraceptive pill. Before that, Central Americans used wild yam root to relieve labor pains. The Chinese species, *Dioscorea opposita*, is used in traditional medicine for breathing difficulties.

Folklore, Superstition, Magic: These roots grow very long, sometimes up to a yard each, which associates them with abundance. Carve into a piece of root a symbol of that which you need to increase and plant it back in the ground. See what grows! Some people believe that eating yams will inspire passion.

Medicinal: Ancient Aztecs and Mayans used this herb as a pain reliever. North and Central American tribes used wild yam to regulate menstrual problems, and in modern times, a decoction is recommended for cramps, while a tincture twice daily is good for achy joints.

Culinary, Crafts: Cultivated yams are grown in the southern states, predominantly Florida. They can be cooked like potatoes and squash or candied as part of holiday meals. A recipe from

Senegal uses yams as a stuffing base mixed with tomato and pineapple, and then seasoned with onion and pepper.

Gardening, Habitat: Wild yam grows natively in the forests of North America but can also grow in semitropical regions. It may be cultivated from seeds or tuber cuttings. It should be planted come spring in a sunny location for a fall harvest of the tubers and roots.

Other: The West Indian name for yam is *nyami,* meaning "to eat."

Willow
Salix alba

Folk Names: Catkin willow, enchanter's tree, aspirin tree

History: The word *saileach* is Gaelic for willow and means "of the sea." The Jewish Feast of the Tabernacles was also called the Day of the Willows. The Romans used willow branches to bind grapevines. During the time of Cato, willows were considered a valuable crop, second only to wine grapes. George Washington planted willows at Mount Vernon.

Folklore, Superstition, Magic: Nicholas Culpeper tells us that willows are a lunar tree, and Robert Graves indicates that willow comprises the fifth letter of the Celtic tree alphabet. In Europe, many believe that the term *Wicca* or *witch* may have some association with the name of this tree, since the willow is associated with magic, charms, and divination.

Carry a piece of willow wood for love or protection. Willow is also associated with death and was often planted on grave sites. Drink wine in which the leaves of this tree have been steeped to cool passion and lust. For beautiful hair, adhere a lock of hair to the bowers of this tree.

Medicinal: The English physician and herbalist Culpeper recommended steeping the leaves in wine to treat dandruff. Galen prescribed willow flowers for drying up fluid retention. The willow bark is an effective aspirin substitute. Use two teaspoons of bark to one pint of water. This preparation also has astringent qualities. Steep willow bark in vinegar and dab it on warts and corns to slowly alleviate these conditions.

Culinary, Crafts: Pussy willows are a lovely addition to handcrafted projects. The supple branches of willows make good ropes, wreaths, and baskets when woven together. In Persia, a water is made from pussy willows, which is then distilled and sweetened. This beverage is served cold.

Gardening, Habitat: Willows like cool, moist soil, but can tolerate semidry conditions. Prune this tree regularly to maintain its fullness.

Other: Tannin in willow bark is good for leather work. White willow bark in a decoction is useful as an astringent.

Witch Hazel
Hamamelis virginiana

Folk Names: Winterbloom, snapping hazelnut, spotted alder

History: Witch hazel derives its name from an Old English word for flexible because the wood was often used in making bows. Up to one hundred years ago, branches from this bush were favored for divining rods to search for water, treasure, and even witches!

Folklore, Superstition, Magic: If you're sad due to a recent breakup, carry a sprig of this bush with you to heal your heart. It will also keep your passions in check. Generally, witch hazel is regarded as a protective talisman.

Medicinal: Witch hazel has numerous uses for the home herbalist to enjoy. When distilled, the resulting fluid is a good skin toner and astringent. Apply this in lotion form to treat acne, hemorrhoids, and bug bites. A good lotion can be made easily by buying pre-prepared tincture at any drugstore and mixing it with an unscented hypoallergenic moisturizer.

Pour a little tincture in your bathwater to relieve skin conditions. Alternatively, boil the bark, twigs, and leaves together and mix them into a cream for a very effective bruise ointment with an anti-inflammatory quality. A witch hazel poultice is an old Native American remedy for bruises and skin irritations.

Culinary, Crafts: The leaves of this bush are lovely and can be waxed to add them to various arrangements.

Gardening, Habitat: This plant grows wild in Canada and in the eastern United States. It prefers a mix of sun and shade and damp sandy soil. If sand isn't readily available, use peat instead. The leaves are best gathered in early fall and distilled for an astringent, along with the bark, which is used in tinctures and ointments.

Other: In the language of flowers, witch hazel represents being spellbound.

———

Woodruff
Asperula odorata

Folk Names: Master of the wood, sweet woodruff, herb waiter, waldmeister, squinancywort, wodrove (fifteenth century)

History: Some evidence suggests woodruff was a festival flower used in celebrations honoring Flora in Rome. During the Middle Ages, people hung the blossoms in churches during holiday observances. Woodruff gets its name from a French term, *roue,* meaning "wheel," due to the way its leaves form around the stem.

Folklore, Superstition, Magic: Carry a piece of woodruff to keep conversations cordial. When grown near the home, woodruff promises prosperity, success, and protection from all harm.

Medicinal: Steep the flowers in oil, then use this mixture to make a cream for minor wounds and boils (see Chapter Two). Woodruff tea alleviates insomnia and nervousness, and it also acts as a gentle liver tonic. Fresh macerated leaves may be applied to minor wounds.

Culinary, Crafts: Woodruff blossoms may be used in soups, salads, vinegars, and sauces. They may also be candied to serve as after-dinner breath fresheners, with a flavor that resembles vanilla mixed with tarragon.

By far, woodruff's most predominant use has been in May Day wine. To prepare it, pour a bottle of wine over a bundle of flowers, allowing the mixture to sit for thirty minutes. Take out the flowers, then mix the wine with a little sugar and sliced oranges. Chill well. Serve with the flowers as a garnish.

Its roots yield a red dye while the stems and leaves produce tan colors when mixed with alum.

Gardening, Habitat: Woodruff prefers a heavy supply of water, loamy soil, and shady locations. Flowers appear in May and June, giving off a vanilla aroma.

Other: Place dry woodruff flowers in a sachet with your linens for a lovely scent that deters insects. In the language of flowers, woodruff represents modesty or humility.

Wormwood
Artemisia absinthium

Folk Names: Absinthe

History: Egyptian records dating back to 1600 BCE note wormwood as a cure for worms. During the Middle Ages, people used pieces of wormwood to keep moths out of clothing. Some Mexicans wore wormwood when honoring the salt goddess.

Wormwood was once a popular flavoring for vermouth and other alcoholic beverages, but it is now illegal due to its negative side effects. It is toxic in large quantities and can cause retching.

Folklore, Superstition, Magic: Legend has it that wormwood sprang from the serpent's tail as it hastily left the Garden of Eden. The Anglo-Saxons administered wormwood to alleviate the deadly effects of hemlock. Mystically, wormwood acts as an amulet of protection from witchcraft, but also improves psychic abilities when carried or worn.

Medicinal: Wormwood is used as a worm purgative and digestive aid that decreases flatulence. When used cautiously, it improves overall vigor. It is best made as an infusion. A strong tincture works well for anemia. It should not be consumed when pregnant.

Culinary, Crafts: The greenish gray leaves of this plant look pretty in dried floral bouquets, but take care to keep such an ornamental item far from the reach of children and pets.

Gardening, Habitat: Wormwood is native to Europe and will flourish in most temperate regions. Use it in the garden to deter flea beetles and cabbage worms but keep it a good distance from your plants for this purpose as it can kill them with its toxicity. Harvest the leaves in late summer.

Other: Add wormwood to bug repellent waters or creams. In the language of flowers, this represents absence.

Yarrow
Achillea millefolium

Folk Names: Nosebleed, milfoil, sweet maudlin, sneezewort, green arrow, camil, carpenter grass. Devil's nettle, hundred-leaved grass, spurge olive, spurge flax, wild pepper

History: The Romans called this herb *herba militaris* because healers often applied it to war wounds. The I Ching system of divination developed from yarrow. Its stalks were picked, dried, and casted to form hexagrams.

Folklore, Superstition, Magic: Yarrow was a popular magical herb used to increase an incantation's power. It received its botanical name from Achilles, who used it after Chiron introduced him to its virtues.

The witches of England believed that demons hate this herb. In northern Scotland, people hold a leaf of yarrow to their eyes to see the person of whom they're thinking. Yarrow is also a popular herb in love divination, both in Europe and the United

States, where it is put under a pillow to bring a dream of one's future mate. A stalk of yarrow picked on Midsummer's Eve and put in the home will keep the inhabitants healthy for an entire year. The Saxons used this herb as a general protective amulet.

Medicinal: Yarrow's flowers and leaves are used in teas for colds, flu, colic, hay fever, and menstrual pain. As a remedial tonic, yarrow has a very bitter taste, so consider offsetting its flavor with other herbs such as mint, or a sweetener such as honey. Note that if this tea is used for young children's stomach troubles, honey is not recommended. The flowers make an excellent poultice for minor scrapes and cuts. When steeped in oil and then added to a cream (see Chapter Two), yarrow makes an excellent bruise ointment. Yarrow should not be used when pregnant as it may cause miscarriage.

Culinary, Crafts: In the kitchen, the best use for yarrow is in tea. For crafts, the fronds from this plant look lovely in pressed flower arrangements. In beauty crafts, add yarrow to skin preparations for cleansing.

Gardening, Habitat: Native to Europe and Asia, yarrow grows best in temperate zones, often being mistaken for a weed. It likes rich well-watered soil and is best harvested in summer. Plant yarrow near other aromatics to increase their essential oils.

Other: Parkinson believed that yarrow mixed with olive oil could prevent baldness. Mixed with alum, yarrow yields a yellow dye. In the language of flowers, yarrow represents war.

Yew
Taxus baccata

Folk Names: None.

History: The yew is one of the five magical trees of Ireland used by druids to mark holy sites. Medieval churchyards also favored this tree.

Folklore, Superstition, Magic: The tree's deadly nature is linked to Hekate, the goddess of the underworld. In Druidry, the yew represents immortality, and it is one of the more popular woods for fashioning magic wands in metaphysical traditions.

Medicinal: Although it was used in the past for urinary tract infections and to treat rheumatism, yew is very toxic and unsafe for medicinal use.

Culinary, Crafts: The yew has very ornamental branches with bright red berries, perfect for fashioning wreaths or as part of floral arrangements.

Gardening, Habitat: Yews make excellent hedge and topiary trees. They appreciate both sun and shade and grow well in soil with some humus mixed in.

Other: Yew was a popular wood for bows and dagger handles in the Middle Ages. In the language of flowers, yew represents sorrow.

⸿ *Appendix A* ⸾
Who's Who

Herbalism experienced many global influences, directly or indirectly. While Egyptian, Arabic, Indian, and some other Eastern beliefs inspired European herbals, many of these sources are only now becoming recognized and utilized in Western culture. Consequently, most of the individuals listed here are from the Greco-Roman or European herbal tradition, the most significant authority that shaped Western ideas about the herbal arts.

Aristotle: A Greek philosopher living from 384 to 322 BCE who developed the idea of humors (the four different types of fluids in the body). He then detailed in *De Plantis* which of over 500 herbs should be used for a treatment depending on which of the humors were out of balance.

Bach, Edward: Dr. Edward Bach, a renowned British physician, invented the Bach Flower Essences in the late 1920s as a vibrational type of homeopathy. Each flower essence contains very little of the actual plant because Bach believed plants carry a cellular code that can aid emotional well-being through internalization.

Culpeper, Nicholas: Living in the mid-1600s, Culpeper was an English physician who used his practical experience to write *The English Physician*. This book gives applications for various herbs, their ruling planets, star signs, and observations on how functional their traditional uses seemed to be in his practice.

Dioscorides: A Greek herbalist and physician living from approximately 40 to 90 CE. Dioscorides used Asian and Egyptian sources as the foundation for his writings. The *Materia Medica* logged approximately 500 plants with descriptions, Greek synonyms, habitat, illustrations, preparation instructions, and uses. His work would influence all medicine that followed.

Dodoens, Rembert: A Belgian writer of the 1550s who used fresh plants to illustrate his herbal encyclopedia, along with corresponding recipes.

Fuchs, Leonhart: A German plant historian of the early 1500s who provided illustrated texts to which to refer.

Galen: A Roman physician, philosopher, and teacher living in 130–200 CE who logged approximately 130 different herbal antidotes and medicines in his writings. Galen was inspired by Hippocrates to write hundreds of herbal books. To this day, medicines derived from plants (as opposed to chemical means) are sometimes called *galenicals,* to honor his contribution.

Gerald, John: An herbalist of the late 1500s whose work included the exotic flora and fauna of England. While this was more on horticulture than herbalism, it helped identify plants brought to Europe through merchants and explorers.

Hippocrates: Living from approximately 460–377 BCE, Hippocrates became the Father of Medicine by separating magic from science. Hippocrates classified herbs elementally as *hot, dry, cold,* or *moist.* He also used plant matter, common foods, alum, lead, and copper in some of his treatments.

Matthiolas: An Italian physician of the 1500s who not only wrote about the herbal and medical arts but also sought to uncover the quackery in both sectors of the health community.

Paracelsus: Living from 1493 to 1541, Paracelsus said, "what a doctor needs is a profound knowledge of nature and her works." Taking this to heart, Paracelsus logged exact dosages for herbal preparations, which laid the foundations for both chemistry and holistics.

Parkinson, John: In 1640, Parkinson published *Theatrum Botanicum,* which covered nearly four thousand plants, combining fact with folk wisdom and periodic imaginative tangents.

Pliny: A Roman scholar living from 23 to 79 CE, Pliny compiled thirty-seven books on the herbal arts. He drew on the works of over 400 authors for his *Natural History,* which meticulously recorded popular herbal lore and applications of the time.

Appendix B
Correspondence Listing

Agrimony
  Ruling Planet: *Jupiter*
  Spirits & Deities: *N/A*
  Magical Correspondence: *Safety, Rest*
  Element: *Air*

Alder
  Ruling Planet: *Venus*
  Spirits & Deities: *Bran, Fairies*
  Magical Correspondence: *Resurrection*
  Element: *Water*

Alfafa
  Ruling Planet: *Venus*
  Spirits & Deities: *N/A*
  Magical Correspondence: *Providence, Prosperity*
  Element: *Earth*

Aloe
  Ruling Planet: *Moon*
  Spirits & Deities: *Aphrodite*
  Magical Correspondence: *Beauty, Fortune, Safety*
  Element: *Water*

Angelica
  Ruling Planet: *Sun*
  Spirits & Deities: *N/A*
  Magical Correspondence: *Banishing, Insight*
  Element: *Water*

Anise
> Ruling Planet: *Jupiter*
> Spirits & Deities: *N/A*
> Magical Correspondence: *Youth, Vitality, Rest*
> Element: *Air*

Apple
> Ruling Planet: *Venus*
> Spirits & Deities: *Apollo, Aphrodite, Bran, Diana, Frey, Frigga*
> Magical Correspondence: *Love, Desire, Health*
> Element: *Water*

Ash
> Ruling Planet: *Sun*
> Spirits & Deities: *Achilles, Mars, Odin, Poseidon, Thor, Uranus*
> Magical Correspondence: *Safety, Prosperity, Health, Inspiration*
> Element: *Water, Fire*

Asparagus
> Ruling Planet: *Jupiter, Mars*
> Spirits & Deities: *N/A*
> Magical Correspondence: *Virility*
> Element: *Water, Fire*

Avocado
> Ruling Planet: *Venus*
> Spirits & Deities: *N/A*
> Magical Correspondence: *Passion, Beauty*
> Element: *Water, Earth*

Balm
> Ruling Planet: *Moon*
> Spirits & Deities: *N/A*
> Magical Correspondence: *Victory, Health*
> Element: *Water*

Banana
> Ruling Planet: *Venus, Mars*
> Spirits & Deities: *Kanaloa, Vishnu*
> Magical Correspondence: *Prosperity, Fertility, Luck in Relationships*
> Element: *Water, Air*

Barley

    Ruling Planet: *Saturn*
    Spirits & Deities: *Demeter, Indra, Ra*
    Magical Correspondence: *Fecundity, Prosperity*
    Element: *Earth*

Basil

    Ruling Planet: *Mars*
    Spirits & Deities: *Krishna, Lakshmi, Vishnu*
    Magical Correspondence: *Loyalty, Adoration, Compassion, Prosperity, Joy*
    Element: *Fire*

Bay

    Ruling Planet: *Sun*
    Spirits & Deities: *Apollo, Ceres, Eros*
    Magical Correspondence: *Success, Strength, Victory, Luck, Prophecy*
    Element: *Fire*

Bayberry

    Ruling Planet: *Venus*
    Spirits & Deities: *Aphrodite*
    Magical Correspondence: *Luck, Prophecy, Devotion*
    Element: *Water*

Bean

    Ruling Planet: *Mercury, Venus*
    Spirits & Deities: *Cardea, Demeter, Kachina*
    Magical Correspondence: *Divination, Love, Health*
    Element: *Air*

Beech

    Ruling Planet: *Saturn*
    Spirits & Deities: *Bacchus, Zeus*
    Magical Correspondence: *Luck*
    Element: *Water*

Benzoin

    Ruling Planet: *Sun*
    Spirits & Deities: *N/A*
    Magical Correspondence: *Wishes, Oracles*
    Element: *Air*

Birch
Ruling Planet: *Venus*
Spirits & Deities: *Thor*
Magical Correspondence: *Purification, Abundance*
Element: *Air*

Blue Cohosh
Ruling Planet: *N/A*
Spirits & Deities: *N/A*
Magical Correspondence: *Cleansing, Awareness, Protection, Love, Courage*
Element: *Water*

Borage
Ruling Planet: *Jupiter*
Spirits & Deities: *N/A*
Magical Correspondence: *Valor, Joy, Psychic Powers*
Element: *Air*

Broom
Ruling Planet: *Mars*
Spirits & Deities: *Sao Ching-Niang*
Magical Correspondence: *Weather, Cleansing, Divination*
Element: *Air*

Burdock
Ruling Planet: *Venus*
Spirits & Deities: *N/A*
Magical Correspondence: *Wellness, Safety*
Element: *Water*

Cabbage
Ruling Planet: *Moon*
Spirits & Deities: *Zeus*
Magical Correspondence: *Luck, Money, Garden Magic*
Element: *Water*

Calendula
Ruling Planet: *N/A*
Spirits & Deities: *Fairies*
Magical Correspondence: *Vision, Joy, Dreams*
Element: *Air*

Caraway
 Ruling Planet: *Mercury*
 Spirits & Deities: *N/A*
 Magical Correspondence: *Awareness, Protection, Devotion*
 Element: *Air*

Cardamom
 Ruling Planet: *Venus*
 Spirits & Deities: *Erzulie*
 Magical Correspondence: *Love, Passion*
 Element: *Water*

Carnation
 Ruling Planet: *Sun*
 Spirits & Deities: *Jesus, Jupiter, Mary*
 Magical Correspondence: *Vigor, Protection*
 Element: *Fire*

Carob
 Ruling Planet: *Venus*
 Spirits & Deities: *St. John*
 Magical Correspondence: *Luck*
 Element: *Water*

Carrot
 Ruling Planet: *Mercury, Mars*
 Spirits & Deities: *N/A*
 Magical Correspondence: *Fertility*
 Element: Fire

Catnip
 Ruling Planet: *Sun*
 Spirits & Deities: *N/A*
 Magical Correspondence: *N/A*
 Element: *N/A*

Cayenne
 Ruling Planet: *Sun*
 Spirits & Deities: *N/A*
 Magical Correspondence: *Protection*
 Element: *Fire*

Celery
  Ruling Planet: *Sun, Mercury*
  Spirits & Deities: *N/A*
  Magical Correspondence: *Mind, Psychic Powers*
  Element: *Fire*

Chamomile
  Ruling Planet: *Sun*
  Spirits & Deities: *Ra*
  Magical Correspondence: *Sleep, Love, Money*
  Element: *Water*

Cherry
  Ruling Planet: *Venus*
  Spirits & Deities: *Konohama-Sakura*
  Magical Correspondence: *Love, Divination*
  Element: *Water*

Chicory
  Ruling Planet: *Sun*
  Spirits & Deities: *N/A*
  Magical Correspondence: *Hospitality, Prudence, Overcoming*
  Element: *Air*

Chive
  Ruling Planet: *Mars*
  Spirits & Deities: *N/A*
  Magical Correspondence: *Protection*
  Element: *Fire*

Chrysanthemum
  Ruling Planet: *Sun*
  Spirits & Deities: *Amaterasu, Fairies*
  Magical Correspondence: *Longevity, Energy, Blessing*
  Element: *Fire*

Cinnamon
  Ruling Planet: *Sun*
  Spirits & Deities: *Aphrodite, Dionysus, Venus*
  Magical Correspondence: *Long Life, Passion, Vitality, Awareness*
  Element: *Fire*

Clove

Ruling Planet: *Jupiter*
Spirits & Deities: *N/A*
Magical Correspondence: *Cleansing, Romance, Serenity, Abundance*
Element: *Fire*

Clover

Ruling Planet: *Mercury*
Spirits & Deities: *Rowen, St. Patrick*
Magical Correspondence: *Banishing, Devotion*
Element: *Air*

Comfrey

Ruling Planet: *Saturn*
Spirits & Deities: *N/A*
Magical Correspondence: *Travel, Money*
Element: *Water*

Coriander

Ruling Planet: *Mars*
Spirits & Deities: *N/A*
Magical Correspondence: *Longevity, Health, Love*
Element: *Fire*

Corn

Ruling Planet: *Venus*
Spirits & Deities: *Corn Mother, Muyingwa, Quetzalcoatl*
Magical Correspondence: *Health, Providence, Divination*
Element: *Earth*

Cowslip

Ruling Planet: *Venus*
Spirits & Deities: *Fairies, Freya*
Magical Correspondence: *Youthfulness, Treasure*
Element: *Water*

Cumin

Ruling Planet: *Mars*
Spirits & Deities: *Egyptian gods*
Magical Correspondence: *Banishing, Fidelity*
Element: *Fire*

Daisy
    Ruling Planet: *Venus*
    Spirits & Deities: *Freya, Mary, St. John, Thor*
    Magical Correspondence: *Love, Dedication*
    Element: *Water*

Dandelion
    Ruling Planet: *Jupiter*
    Spirits & Deities: *Apollo, Hekate*
    Magical Correspondence: *Divination, Psychic Vision, Hospitality, Protection*
    Element: *Air*

Dill
    Ruling Planet: *Mercury*
    Spirits & Deities: *Horus*
    Magical Correspondence: *Rest, Money, Passion, Protection*
    Element: *Fire*

Echinacea
    Ruling Planet: *N/A*
    Spirits & Deities: *N/A*
    Magical Correspondence: *Evocation*
    Element: *Air*

Elder
    Ruling Planet: *Venus*
    Spirits & Deities: *Fairies, Christ, The Goddess, Jupiter*
    Magical Correspondence: *Protection, Health, Fortune*
    Element: *Water*

Elm
    Ruling Planet: *Saturn*
    Spirits & Deities: *Fairies, Hoenir, Lodur, Odin, Ut*
    Magical Correspondence: *Love, Safety*
    Element: *Water*

Eucalyptus
    Ruling Planet: *Moon*
    Spirits & Deities: *N/A*
    Magical Correspondence: *Health, Safety*
    Element: *Water*

Fennel
Ruling Planet: *Mercury*
Spirits & Deities: *Adonis, Dionysus, Prometheus*
Magical Correspondence: *Alertness, Protection, Health, Love*
Element: *Fire*

Fig
Ruling Planet: *Jupiter*
Spirits & Deities: *Buddha, Ceres, Dionysus, Isis, Juno, Muhammad, Romulus and Remus*
Magical Correspondence: *Fertility, Wisdom, Insight, Vitality*
Element: *Fire*

Garlic
Ruling Planet: *Mars*
Spirits & Deities: *Hekate, Mars*
Magical Correspondence: *Protection, Healing, Banishing, Strength*
Element: *Fire*

Gentian
Ruling Planet: *Mars*
Spirits & Deities: *N/A*
Magical Correspondence: *Power, Wellness*
Element: *Fire*

Geranium
Ruling Planet: *Venus*
Spirits & Deities: *Muhammad*
Magical Correspondence: *Protection, Love, Fertility*
Element: *Water*

Ginger
Ruling Planet: *Mars*
Spirits & Deities: *Chinese gods*
Magical Correspondence: *Energy, Victory, Prosperity, Love*
Element: *Fire*

Ginseng
Ruling Planet: *Sun*
Spirits & Deities: *N/A*
Magical Correspondence: *Prophecy, Wishes, Passion, Health*
Element: *Fire*

Goldenrod
Ruling Planet: *Venus*
Spirits & Deities: *N/A*
Magical Correspondence: *Divination*
Element: *Air*

Hawthorn
Ruling Planet: *Mars*
Spirits & Deities: *Christ, Flora*
Magical Correspondence: *Fecundity, Joy, Devotion*
Element: *Fire*

Hazel
Ruling Planet: *Sun*
Spirits & Deities: *St. John*
Magical Correspondence: *Knowledge, Luck, Divination, Abundance, Wishes*
Element: *Air*

Heather
Ruling Planet: *Venus*
Spirits & Deities: *Isis*
Magical Correspondence: *Peace, Weather, Beauty, Health*
Element: *Water*

Hickory
Ruling Planet: *Sun*
Spirits & Deities: *N/A*
Magical Correspondence: *Legal Matters, Weather Magic*
Element: *Fire*

Honeysuckle
Ruling Planet: *Jupiter*
Spirits & Deities: *N/A*
Magical Correspondence: *Money, Safety, Luck*
Element: *Earth*

Hops
Ruling Planet: *Mars*
Spirits & Deities: *N/A*
Magical Correspondence: *Rest, Health*
Element: *Air*

Horseradish
Ruling Planet: *Mars*
Spirits & Deities: *N/A*
Magical Correspondence: *Purification, Protection*
Element: *Fire*

Irish Moss
Ruling Planet: *Moon*
Spirits & Deities: *N/A*
Magical Correspondence: *Luck, Protection*
Element: *Water*

Jasmine
Ruling Planet: *Moon*
Spirits & Deities: *Buddha, Diana, Kwan Yin, Vishnu*
Magical Correspondence: *Prosperity, Prophecy, Spiritual Love*
Element: *Water*

Juniper
Ruling Planet: *Sun*
Spirits & Deities: *N/A*
Magical Correspondence: *Exorcism, Psychic Powers, Health, Protection*
Element: *Fire*

Lavender
Ruling Planet: *Mercury*
Spirits & Deities: *Mary*
Magical Correspondence: *Peace, Joy, Love, Wishes*
Element: *Air*

Lemon
Ruling Planet: *Moon*
Spirits & Deities: *N/A*
Magical Correspondence: *Friendship, Cleansing, Devotion*
Element: *Water*

Licorice
Ruling Planet: *Venus*
Spirits & Deities: *N/A*
Magical Correspondence: *Fidelity, Passion*
Element: *Water*

Lilac
Ruling Planet: *Venus*
Spirits & Deities: *N/A*
Magical Correspondence: *Banishing Ghosts*
Element: *Water*

Lily
Ruling Planet: *Moon*
Spirits & Deities: *Dominic, Juno, Mary, Kwan Yin, Venus*
Magical Correspondence: *Hex-Breaking, Purity*
Element: *Water*

Lotus
Ruling Planet: *Moon*
Spirits & Deities: *Agni, Aphrodite, Brahma, Ho Hsien Ku, Horus, Isis, Lakshmi, Osiris, Venus, Vishnu*
Magical Correspondence: *Longevity, Fortune, Fertility, Reincarnation, Virtue*
Element: *Water*

Magnolia
Ruling Planet: *Venus*
Spirits & Deities: *N/A*
Magical Correspondence: *Devotion*
Element: *Earth*

Mandrake
Ruling Planet: *Mercury*
Spirits & Deities: *Aphrodite, Circe, Hekate*
Magical Correspondence: *Fertility, Love, Protection*
Element: *Fire*

Marigold
Ruling Planet: *Mars*
Spirits & Deities: *Fairies, Mahadeva, Mars, Mary, Vishnu*
Magical Correspondence: *Justice, Oracles, Comfort*
Element: *Air*

Marjoram
Ruling Planet: *Mercury*
Spirits & Deities: *Aphrodite, Ilmarinen, Osiris, Venus, Vishnu*
Magical Correspondence: *Love, Joy, Safety, Abundance*
Element: *Air*

Marsh Mallow
Ruling Planet: *Moon*
Spirits & Deities: *N/A*
Magical Correspondence: *Protection, Love, Banishing*
Element: *Water*

Meadowsweet
Ruling Planet: *Jupiter*
Spirits & Deities: *Blodeuwedd, Llew*
Magical Correspondence: *Peace, Joy, Discernment*
Element: *Air*

Mint
Ruling Planet: *Venus*
Spirits & Deities: *Hekate, Persephone, Pluto, St. John*
Magical Correspondence: *Refreshment, Safe Travel, Passion, Joy, Well-Being, Virility, Hospitality*
Element: *Air*

Mistletoe
Ruling Planet: *Sun*
Spirits & Deities: *Apollo, Freya, Odin*
Magical Correspondence: *Conception, Safety, Love, Luck*
Element: *Air*

Mugwort
Ruling Planet: *Venus*
Spirits & Deities: *Artemis, Diana, St. John*
Magical Correspondence: *Dreams, Insight, Stamina, Fertility*
Element: *Earth*

Mulberry
Ruling Planet: *Mercury*
Spirits & Deities: *Diana, Minerva*
Magical Correspondence: *Vitality, Protection, Prudence, Patience*
Element: *Air*

Mustard
Ruling Planet: *Sun*
Spirits & Deities: *Asclepius, Mars*
Magical Correspondence: *Health, Conscious Mind, Fruitfulness, Faith*
Element: *Fire*

Myrrh
Ruling Planet: *Moon*
Spirits & Deities: *Isis, Ra*
Magical Correspondence: *Cleansing, Prayer*
Element: *Water*

Nasturtium
Ruling Planet: *Neptune*
Spirits & Deities: *N/A*
Magical Correspondence: *Conviction, Celebration, Luck, Energy*
Element: *Air*

Nettle
Ruling Planet: *Mars*
Spirits & Deities: *Fabian, Thor*
Magical Correspondence: *Passion, Safety, Health*
Element: *Fire*

Nutmeg
Ruling Planet: *Jupiter*
Spirits & Deities: *N/A*
Magical Correspondence: *Fortune, Prosperity, Devotion, Vision*
Element: *Fire*

Oak
Ruling Planet: *Sun*
Spirits & Deities: *Angels, Cybele, Dagda, Hekate, Juno, Jupiter, Pan, Rhea, Silvanus, Zeus*
Magical Correspondence: *Finances, Strength, Abundance, Nature, Weather Magic, Longevity*
Element: *Fire*

Oat
Ruling Planet: *Venus*
Spirits & Deities: *Ceres, Demeter*
Magical Correspondence: *Providence, Money, Fertile Land*
Element: *Earth*

Olive
Ruling Planet: *Sun*
Spirits & Deities: *Athena, Minerva, Ra*
Magical Correspondence: *Healing, Peace, Fertility*
Element: *Fire*

Onion
Ruling Planet: *Mars*
Spirits & Deities: *Isis, St. Thomas*
Magical Correspondence: *Longevity, Protection*
Element: *Fire*

Orange
Ruling Planet: *Sun*
Spirits & Deities: *Hera, Zeus*
Magical Correspondence: *Devotion, Fortune, Purity*
Element: *Fire*

Orchid
Ruling Planet: *Venus*
Spirits & Deities: *Orchis, Venus*
Magical Correspondence: *Love, Passion*
Element: *Water*

Pansy
Ruling Planet: *Saturn*
Spirits & Deities: *N/A*
Magical Correspondence: *Romance, Weather Magic*
Element: *Water*

Parsley
Ruling Planet: *Mercury*
Spirits & Deities: *Persephone*
Magical Correspondence: *Security, Sensuality, Cleansing*
Element: *Air*

Pine
Ruling Planet: *Mars*
Spirits & Deities: *Astarte, Dionysus, Pan, Sylvanus, Venus*
Magical Correspondence: *Cleansing, Prosperity, Safety, Fertility, Long Life*
Element: *Air*

Pineapple
Ruling Planet: *Sun*
Spirits & Deities: *N/A*
Magical Correspondence: *Hospitality, Money, Luck*
Element: *Fire*

Pomegranate
Ruling Planet: *Mercury*
Spirits & Deities: *Ceres, Persephone*
Magical Correspondence: *Fertility, Wishes, Divination*
Element: *Fire*

Poplar
Ruling Planet: *Saturn*
Spirits & Deities: *Calypso, Hercules*
Magical Correspondence: *Communication, Divination, Time*
Element: *Water*

Pumpkin
Ruling Planet: *Moon*
Spirits & Deities: *N/A*
Magical Correspondence: *Protection*
Element: *Water*

Quince
Ruling Planet: *Saturn*
Spirits & Deities: *Venus*
Magical Correspondence: *Safety, Promises*
Element: *Earth*

Radish
Ruling Planet: *Mars*
Spirits & Deities: *N/A*
Magical Correspondence: *Passion, Overcoming*
Element: *Fire*

Raspberry
Ruling Planet: *Venus*
Spirits & Deities: *N/A*
Magical Correspondence: *Abundance, Adoration*
Element: *Water*

Rose
Ruling Planet: *Venus*
Spirits & Deities: *Aphrodite, Cupid, Demeter, Eros, Hathor*
Magical Correspondence: *Love, Luck, Psychic Energy, Health*
Element: *Water*

Rosemary
Ruling Planet: *Sun*
Spirits & Deities: *Mary*
Magical Correspondence: *Remembrance, Love, Health, Rest and Energy*
Element: *Fire*

Rowan
Ruling Planet: *Sun*
Spirits & Deities: *Thor*
Magical Correspondence: *Divination, Protection, Health*
Element: *Fire*

Saffron
Ruling Planet: *Sun*
Spirits & Deities: *Amun Ra, Ashtoreth, Brahma, Eos*
Magical Correspondence: *Love, Prosperity, Strength, Mystical Insight, Passion, Joy*
Element: *Fire*

Sage
Ruling Planet: *Jupiter*
Spirits & Deities: *Jupiter, Zeus*
Magical Correspondence: *Wisdom, Longevity, Wishes, Fertility, Prudence*
Element: *Air*

St. John's Wort
Ruling Planet: *Sun*
Spirits & Deities: *Baldur*
Magical Correspondence: *Vigor, Well-Being, Joy, Psychic Abilities, Love Divination*
Element: *Fire*

Savory
Ruling Planet: *Mercury*
Spirits & Deities: *N/A*
Magical Correspondence: *Passion, Awareness*
Element: *Air*

Strawberry
Ruling Planet: *Venus*
Spirits & Deities: *Fairies, Frigga, Mary*
Magical Correspondence: *Luck, Abundance*
Element: *Water*

Sweet Flag
Ruling Planet: *N/A*
Spirits & Deities: *N/A*
Magical Correspondence: *Passion*
Element: *N/A*

Tansy
Ruling Planet: *Venus*
Spirits & Deities: *Venus*
Magical Correspondence: *Well-Being, Longevity*
Element: *Water*

Tarragon
Ruling Planet: *Mars*
Spirits & Deities: *Ganymede*
Magical Correspondence: *Power, Zest*
Element: *Fire*

Thyme
Ruling Planet: *Venus, Mars*
Spirits & Deities: *Fairies*
Magical Correspondence: *Fairy Sight, Sleep, Bravery, Health*
Element: *Water*

Tomato
Ruling Planet: *Venus*
Spirits & Deities: *N/A*
Magical Correspondence: *Love, Fortune*
Element: *Water*

Tumeric
Ruling Planet: *N/A*
Spirits & Deities: *N/A*
Magical Correspondence: *Cleansing*
Element: *N/A*

Valerian
Ruling Planet: *Venus*
Spirits & Deities: *N/A*
Magical Correspondence: *Calming, Communion, Lust*
Element: *Water*

Vervain
Ruling Planet: *Venus*
Spirits & Deities: *Aradia, Christ, Jupiter, Mithra, Venus, Zeus*
Magical Correspondence: *Anti-Magic, Prophecy, Love, Luck*
Element: *Earth*

Violet
Ruling Planet: *Venus*
Spirits & Deities: *Cupid, Venus*
Magical Correspondence: *Luck, Wishes, Ghost Protection, Love*
Element: *Water*

Walnut
Ruling Planet: *Sun*
Spirits & Deities: *Greek gods*
Magical Correspondence: *Protection, Mental Keenness*
Element: *Fire*

Watermelon
Ruling Planet: *Moon*
Spirits & Deities: *Set, Yemaya*
Magical Correspondence: *Weight Gain*
Element: *Water*

Wild Yam
Ruling Planet: *Venus*
Spirits & Deities: *N/A*
Magical Correspondence: *Plenty*
Element: *Water*

Willow
Ruling Planet: *Moon*
Spirits & Deities: *Artemis, Ceres, Hera, Hekate, Mercury, Persephone*
Magical Correspondence: *Divination, Health, Safety, Romance*
Element: *Water*

Witch Hazel
Ruling Planet: *Sun*
Spirits & Deities: *N/A*
Magical Correspondence: *Devotion, Protection, Decreased Passion*
Element: *Fire*

Woodruff

Ruling Planet: *Mars*
Spirits & Deities: *N/A*
Magical Correspondence: *Success, Prosperity, Cordial Feelings*
Element: *Fire*

Wormwood

Ruling Planet: *Mars*
Spirits & Deities: *Artemis, Salt goddess*
Magical Correspondence: *Anti-Magic, Psychic Powers*
Element: *Fire*

Yarrow

Ruling Planet: *Venus*
Spirits & Deities: *Achilles*
Magical Correspondence: *Divination, Protection, Power, Health*
Element: *Water*

Yew

Ruling Planet: *Saturn*
Spirits & Deities: *Hekate*
Magical Correspondence: *Resurrection, Longevity*
Element: *Water*

Appendix C

Herbs by Name

Bibliography

Ainsworth-Davis, James R. *Cooking Through the Centuries*. Jim Dent and Sons, 1931.

Arnold, John E. *Origin and History of Beer and Brewing*. Wahl-Henius Institute of Fermentology, 1911.

Beyerl, Paul. *Master Book of Herbalism*. Phoenix Publishing, 1984.

Black, William George. *Folk Medicine*. Burt Franklin, 1883.

Buckland, Raymond. *Gypsy Love Magic*. Llewellyn Publications, 1992.

Budge, Sir Ernest Wallis. *Herb Doctors and Physicians in the Ancient World*. Ares Publishing, 1978.

Chase, A. W, M.D. *Practical Recipes*. R.A. Beal, 1870.

——. *Receipt Book and Household Physician*. F. B. Dickerson Co., 1908.

Chevallier, Andrew. *Encyclopedia of Medicinal Plants*. DK Publishing, 1996.

Clarkson, Rosetta. *The Golden Age of Herbs and Herbalists*. Dover Publishing, 1940.

——. *Herbs and Savory Seeds*. Dover Publishing, 1972.

Conway, D. J. *Ancient Shining Ones*. Llewellyn Publications, 1993.

Cooley, Arnold J. *Handbook of the Toilet*. J. B. Lippincott and Co., 1873.

Cristiani, R. S. *Perfumery and Kindred Arts*. Sampson Low Publishing, 1877.

Culpeper, Nicholas. *English Physician*. Meyerbooks, 1990.

Cunningham, Scott. *Cunningham's Encyclopedia of Magical Herbs*. Llewellyn Publications, 1985.

——. *The Magic in Food*. Llewellyn Publications, 1991.

Dyer, T. E. *Folklore of Plants*. D. Appleton & Co., 1889.

Emerson, Ralph Waldo. *Eulogy of May 9th, 1862*. Atlantic Monthly, 1862.

Farrar, Janet and Stewart Farrar. *The Witches' God*. Phoenix Publishing, 1989.

—. *The Witches' Goddess*. Phoenix Publishing, 1987.

Fox, Dr. William. *Family Botanical Guide*. Wm. Fox and Sons, 1907.

Freethy, Ron. *Book of Plant Uses, Names, and Folklore*. Tanager Books, 1985.

Gordon, Leslie. *Green Magic*. Viking Press, 1977.

Gordon, Stuart. *The Encyclopedia of Myths and Legends*. Headline Book Publishing, 1994.

Griggs, B. *History of Herbal Medicine*. New York: Viking Press, 1981.

Harlan, William. *Illustrated History of Eating and Drinking through the Ages*. American Heritage Publishers, 1968.

Hechtlinger, Adelaide. *The Seasonal Hearth*. Overlook Press, 1986.

Hiss, Emil. *Standard Manual of Soda and Other Beverages*. G. R Englehand & Co., 1897.

Hoffman, David. *Herbalism*. Element Books, 1990.

Hopkins, Albert. *Home Made Beverages*. Scientific American Publishing Co., 1919.

Hottes, Alfred C. *The Book of Perennials*. A. T. DeLaMare Co., 1933.

—. *The Book of Shrubs*. A. T. DeLaMare Co., 1931.

—. *The Book of Trees*. A.T. DeLaMare Co., 1932.

Hutchison, Ruth and Ruth Adams. *Every Day's a Holiday*. Harper Brothers, 1951.

Hylton, William H., ed. *The Rodale Herb Book*. Rodale Press Book, 1974.

Ickis, Marguerite. *Book of Festival Holidays*. Dodd, Mead, 1964.

Jagendorf, M. A. *Folk Wines*. Vanguard Press, 1963.

Kieckhefer, R. *Magic in the Middle Ages*. Cambridge University Press, 1989.

Kowalchik, Claire and William H. Hylton, eds. *Kodak's Illustrated Encyclopedia of Herbs*. Rodale Press, 1987.

Leach, Maria, ed. *Folklore, Mythology, and Legend*. Harper & Row, 1972.

LeStrainge, R. *History of Herbal Plants*. Aroc Publishing, 1977.

Louisa, Patricia. *Cooking with Herbs*. Bloomsbury Books, 1988.

MacNicol, Mary. *Flower Cookery*. Fleet Press Corporation, 1967.

McHoy, Peter and Pamela Westland. *The Herb Bible*. Barnes & Noble Books, 1995.

Metcalfe, Joannah. *Herbs and Aromatherapy*. Bloomsbury Press, 1993.

Meyer, Joseph E. *The Herbalist*. Clarence Meyer, 2016.

Mone, Amy, and Valerie Mehl. "Intravenous Mistletoe Extract Shows Promise as Cancer Therapy in Small Study." *Alternative Medicine*, John Hopkins University, 23 Feb. 2023, www.hub.jhu.edu/2023/02/23/mistletoe-extract-cancer-treatment-study/.

Murray, Michael T. *The Healing Power of Herbs*. Prima Publishing, 1992.

Mystical Year. Mysteries of the Unknown series. Time-Life Books, 1992.

Northcote, Lady Rosaline. *Book of Herb Lore*. Dover Publishing, 1912.

Palaiseul, Jean. *Grandmother's Secrets*. G. P. Putnam's Sons, 1974.

Paulson, Kathryn. *Magic and Witchcraft*. Pentacle Press, 1980.

Peterson, Nicola. *Herbs and Health*. Bloomsbury Books, 1989.

Potterton, D., ed. *Culpeper's Herbal*. Sterling Publishing, 1983.

Riotte, Louise. *Sleeping with a Sunflower*. Garden Way Publishing, 1987.

Rohde, Eleanour S. *Olde English Herbals*. Dover Publishing, 1922.

Ronm, Aviva Jill. *The Natural Pregnancy Book*. Crossing Press, 1997.

Schapira, David. *Book of Coffee and Tea*. St. Martin's Press, 1906.

Seymour, E. L. D., ed. *The Garden Encyclopedia*. Wm. H. Wise & Co., 1936.

Sheen, Joanna. *Flower Crafts*. Salamander Books, 1992.

Singer, C. *From Magic to Science*. Dover Publishing, 1928.

Skinner, Charles M. *Myths and Legends of Flowers, Trees, Fruits and Plants*. Lippincott, 1925.

Soule, Deb. *The Roots of Healing*. Carol Publishing Group, 1995.

Stary, Frantisek. *Medicinal Herbs and Plants*. Dorset Press, 1991.

Summerrain, Mary. *Earthway*. Pocketbooks, 1990.

Tannahill, Reay. *Food in History*. Stein & Day, 1973.

Telesco, Patricia. *Kitchen Witch's Cookbook*. Llewellyn Publications, 1994.

—. *Witch's Brew*. Lewellyn Publications, 1995.

Turgeon, Charlotte. *Encyclopedia of Creative Cooking*. Weathervane Books, 1982.

Vargas, Pattie and Rich Gulling. *Country Wines*. Garden Way Publishing, 1992.

Vukovic, Laurel. *Naturally Beautiful*. Herbal Alchemy, 1997.

Williams, Jude. *Jude's Herbal*. Llewellyn Publications, 1992.

Woodward, Marcus, ed. *Gerard's Herball*. Bracken Books, 1985.

Worwood, Valerie Ann. *The Complete Book of Essential Oils and Aromatherapy*. New World Library, 1991.

Williams, Jude. *Jude's Herbal*. Llewellyn Publications, 1992.

Woodward, Marcus, ed. *Gerard's Herbal*. Bracken Books, 1985.

Worwood, Valerie Ann. *The Complete Book of Essential Oils and Aromatherapy*. New World Library, 1991.